HEINEMANN
Integrated Skills
elementary
Workbook
with answer key

**MARGARET CALLOW
AND PHILIP PROWSE**

Heinemann International
A division of Heinemann Educational Books Ltd
Halley Court, Jordan Hill, Oxford OX2 8EJ

OXFORD LONDON EDINBURGH
MADRID ATHENS BOLOGNA PARIS
MELBOURNE SYDNEY AUCKLAND SINGAPORE TOKYO
IBADAN NAIROBI HARARE GABORONE
PORTSMOUTH (NH)

ISBN 0 435 28249 2

© Margaret Callow and Philip Prowse 1991

First published 1991

All rights reserved; no part of this publication may be reproduced, stored in a retrieval system, or transmitted in any form or by any means, electronic, mechanical, photocopying, recording, or otherwise, without the prior written permission of the publishers.

Illustrations by
Gecko Ltd. pp 4, 14, 15, 30, 61
Tim Howe pp 9, 25
Sally Launder p 39
Dave Mostyn pp 18, 20, 26, 28, 51
John Plumb p 6
Chris Rothero pp 19, 33, 34, 40, 56
Jacky Rough pp 13, 16, 21, 24, 26, 36, 38, 45
Martin Saunders p 35
Caroline Smith pp 31, 32

Cover by David Brancaleone

Printed and bound in Great Britain by Thomson Litho Ltd., East Kilbride, Scotland

91 92 93 94 95 96 10 9 8 7 6 5 4 3 2 1

Contents

UNIT 1
Lesson 1 — 1
Lesson 2 — 3
Lesson 3 — 5

UNIT 2
Lesson 4 — 7
Lesson 5 — 9
Lesson 6 — 11

UNIT 3
Lesson 7 — 13
Lesson 8 — 15
Lesson 9 — 17

UNIT 4
Lesson 10 — 19
Lesson 11 — 21
Lesson 12 — 23

UNIT 5
Lesson 13 — 25
Lesson 14 — 27
Lesson 15 — 29

UNIT 6
Lesson 16 — 31
Lesson 17 — 33
Lesson 18 — 35

UNIT 7
Lesson 19 — 37
Lesson 20 — 39
Lesson 21 — 41

UNIT 8
Lesson 22 — 43
Lesson 23 — 45
Lesson 24 — 47

UNIT 9
Lesson 25 — 49
Lesson 26 — 51
Lesson 27 — 53

UNIT 10
Lesson 28 — 55
Lesson 29 — 57
Lesson 30 — 59

Key — 61

UNIT 1 LESSON 1

Present Simple Question Formation, Present Simple or Past Simple, Countries, , Furniture and Rooms, Punctuation, Listening.

GRAMMAR

1 Present Simple Question Formation

Make questions using these words.
colour size shape

a ─────────── The blind is red.

b ─────────── The table is octagonal.

c ─────────── The rug is large.

d ─────────── The bookcase is red.

e ─────────── The room is square.

f ─────────── The box is small.

2 Present Simple or Past Simple Tense

Put the verbs in brackets into the right tense.

I ____ (get) this cushion many years ago - I _____ (buy) it in central Greece and it ____ (be) the same red colour as other things in my room. It _____ (echo) the colour of my rug which ____ (be) the central thing in the room. The wooden boxes _____ (not look) very good when I ____ (get) them but I ____ (clean) them up myself and now they _____ (look) great. The desk (be) really my music cupboard - I _____ (keep) my cassettes in it. The eight-sided table is very special - I _____ (buy) it because I already _____ (have) octagonal plates! It _____ (be) a strange shape but I ____ (like) it.

VOCABULARY

3 Countries

Match the capital city with a country from the list below and say what language is spoken there.

Example *Tokyo/Japan/Japanese*

a Ankara ───────────
b Athens ───────────
c Beijing ───────────
d Brasilia ───────────
e Buenos Aires ───────────
f Cairo ───────────
g Copenhagen ───────────
h Madrid ───────────
i Moscow ───────────
j Paris ───────────
k Rome ───────────

Russia   Turkey   Italy
Egypt   Greece   Denmark
Brazil   China   Spain
Argentina   France

LESSON 1 UNIT 1

4 Furniture and Rooms

Put the furniture into columns. Add any other pieces of furniture that you know.

Example bedroom
bed

bathroom	bedroom	dining room	kitchen	living room

bookcase table sink wardrobe cooker
toilet sofa desk

how about the futon

_____

that's japanese of course

_____

why do you like red

_____

because it's a warm colour I suppose why are you asking me all these questions

_____

_____

I don't know I'm just curious

_____

PUNCTUATION

5 Put in capital letters, commas and question marks.

Example is it a desk
Is it a desk?

what do you use it for

_____

it's a music cupboard actually

_____

is it english

_____

no greek

_____

do you like greek things

_____

very much the rug is greek too

_____

LISTENING

6 Listen to the first part of the interview with Corinne on the cassette. Fill in the missing words.

CORINNE There's a lot of red _____ my room. It's my _____ colour and I like it _____ because it makes the room very _____ . I've got a red futon and red spot _____ , a red blind _____ makes the room very _____ I've also got red supports _____ my book shelves so it takes _____ the same colour scheme _____ .

INTERVIEWER And there's _____ cushion on the box _____ down there.

CORINNE This is a cushion _____ Greece which I _____ many years _____ .

UNIT 1 LESSON 2

2 Present Simple, Present Continuous, Times of the Day, Parts of the Body, Time.

GRAMMAR

1 Present Simple   Habit

Put the verbs in brackets into the right tense.

> Anna _____ (get) up at seven o'clock and then she _____ (go) to work. After the guests _____ (check) out, the hotel _____ (be) quiet so then she can write her essays. At lunch time, which _____ (be) one o'clock, she _____ (get) her money and she _____ (have) an hour's lunch break, so then she _____ (go) to the shop and _____ (buy) things for the evening. Then she _____ (go) home for lunch.

2 Present Continuous   Future

Put the verbs in brackets into the right tense: present continuous or present simple.

I usually _____ (have) lunch every day at 12.30, but tomorrow I _____ (work) until 2.00. At 2.00 I _____ (see) an old friend of mine. He _____ (be) also an archaeologist but _____ (not work) in Cambridge. He _____ (come) all the way from Manchester to see me. He _____ (visit) the museum to see our skeletons. He _____ (work) in a museum in Manchester and his main interest _____ (be) bones. He _____ (arrive) at 2.00 because he has a meeting in London first.

VOCABULARY

3 Times of the Day

Match the meal time and greeting with the time of day.

Example 7.30am breakfast
             Good morning

Meals   tea lunch breakfast dinner
             coffee and biscuits cocoa

Greetings Good morning
              Good afternoon
              Good evening
              Good night

Times

7.30am _____

11am _____

1pm. _____

4pm _____

7.30pm _____

11pm _____

3

LESSON 2 UNIT 1

4 Parts of the Body

Match the numbers with the parts of the body.

ankle ☐   knee ☐
elbow ☐   neck ☐
finger ☐   thigh ☐
heel ☐   thumb ☐
toe ☐   wrist ☐

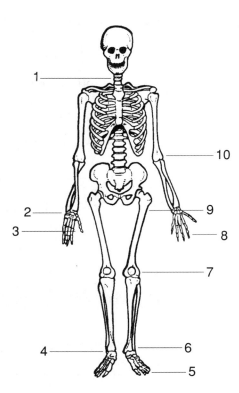

PREPOSITIONS

5 Time

Fill in the missing prepositions.

in   at   to   for   past   from

I usually get up _____ about half _____ six _____ the morning. I have a shower _____ ten minutes or so and then get breakfast. After eating I get ready for work and leave _____ half _____ seven. I catch my bus twenty minutes later _____ ten _____ eight. The bus gets to town _____ twenty five _____ eight and I walk _____ twenty minutes to the office. I usually get to the office _____ a quarter _____ nine and never later than five _____ nine. I have to be at work by nine. I work _____ nine _____ five and then go home. _____ the summer I get up earlier _____ the morning and go to bed later _____ night. That's because I usually try to sleep a little _____ the afternoon.

4

UNIT 1 LESSON 3

3 Comparison of Adjectives, Present Perfect, Sporting Activities, Families, Capital Letters.

GRAMMAR

1 Comparison of Adjectives

Put the adjectives in brackets into the correct form.

Example *The Pacific is the (large) ocean in the world. It is much (large) than the Atlantic Ocean.*
*The Pacific is the **largest** ocean in the world. It is much **larger** than the Atlantic Ocean*

a The _____ (high) mountain in Europe is El'brus in the USSR which is 835 metres _____ (high) than Mont Blanc.

b Australasia is the _____ (small) continent, but few people know that Antartica is _____ (large) than Europe.

c The third _____ (long) river in the world is the Yangtze in China. The _____ (long) is the Nile in Africa, which is 180 kilometres _____ (long) than the Amazon in South America.

d Greenland is nearly ten times (large) _____ than Great Britain and is the (large) _____ island in the world.

e New York, with a population of 17,687,000, is the _____ (big) city in North and Central America, but Mexico City is only a little _____ (small) and its population is growing _____ (fast).

2 Present Perfect   Indefinite Past

Write the questions using the correct form of these verbs.

hear   read   see   try   visit

Example *Dallas is my favourite TV programme. Have you seen it?*

a Madonna is my favourite singer.

_____?

b Computer programming is fun.

_____?

c Switzerland is a beautiful country.

_____?

d *Back to the Future* is the film I like best.

_____?

e I like *A Perfect Spy* by John Le Carré.

_____?

VOCABULARY

3 Sporting Activities and Places

Use words from this list to complete the sentences.

courses   courts   gymnasium   pitch
pools   ring

a The most famous tennis _____ in the world are at Wimbledon.

b Most large towns have swimming _____.

c St Andrew's is one of the best known golf _____ in Scotland.

d You can do aerobics anywhere but a _____ is the best place.

e Many World Title boxing matches have been held in the _____ at Madison Square Garden.

f Wembley is England's best loved football _____ .

4 Families

Complete the sentences using these words.

aunt   cousin   grandfather
grandmother   husband   mother
sister   uncle

a My father is my mother's _____ .
b My mother's daughter is my _____ .
c My mother or father's brother is my _____ .
d My mother or father's sister is my _____ .
e My father's wife is my _____ .
f My uncle and aunt's child is my _____ .
g My father and mother's parents are my _____ and _____

SPELLING

5 Capital Letters

Rewrite this profile putting in capital letters and punctuation where necessary.

description

mario is twenty and comes from turin in northern italy he was born on the first of january and each year has a combined birthday and new year party mario's friends say he has a good sense of humour

likes

he likes discos hamburgers and alpha romeo cars

hobbies

mario speaks english and german as well as italian and has visited most european countries his favourite sport is volleyball he plays the guitar and his favourite group are roxette who come from Sweden

family

he has two brothers attilio and luigi

work

mario is a student at rome university he is studying engineering and wants to work for fiat

UNIT 2 — LESSON 4

Like and Would like, Comparison of Adjectives, Word Puzzle, Education in England.

GRAMMAR

1 Like and Would Like

Examples Yuko **likes** sitting on the floor.
Yuko **would like** to go to America.

Complete with the correct form of *like* or *would like*.

Andreas is fifteen years old and comes from Greece. He _____ swimming and learning English. He is learning English because he _____ to be a doctor. He _____ to study medicine because he _____ helping people. 'I _____ science and mathematics,' Andreas told me, 'but I (not) _____ to be a scientist. I _____ to specialise in paediatrics because I _____ being with children.' In his spare time Andreas _____ dancing as well as swimming, and _____ to learn to fly.

2 Comparison of Irregular and Longer Adjectives

Example Yuko finds studying with her friends **more effective** than working by herself. She finds this **best**.

Complete with the correct form of the adjectives in brackets.

Isabelle writes _____ (good) in the morning before breakfast. She uses her dictionary a lot and has the _____ (expensive) dictionary in the class. Jorge thinks working in his room is _____ (useful) than using the library. He works _____ (good) between seven and nine in the evening. Ahmed is the _____ (good) in the class at speaking and the _____ (bad) at writing. He is _____ (thoughtful) than the other students and is always ready to help them. Isabelle spends the _____ (more) time studying and Jorge the _____ (less). You do your _____ (good) when you are relaxed. Being relaxed is _____ (important) than anything else.

LESSON 4 UNIT 2

VOCABULARY

3 Use the clues to complete the words.

Reply	A _ _ _ _ _
First Meal	B _ _ _ _ _ _ _ _
Dark drink	C _ _ _ _ _
Word book	D _ _ _ _ _ _ _ _ _
End of day	E _ _ _ _ _ _
People who like me	F _ _ _ _ _ _
Capital: Athens	G _ _ _ _ _
Private study	H _ _ _ _ _ _ _
Not boring	I _ _ _ _ _ _ _ _ _ _
Capital: Tokyo	J _ _ _ _
Middle of leg	K _ _ _
Place for study	L _ _ _ _ _ _
First weekday	M _ _ _ _ _
Not day	N _ _ _ _
My view	O _ _ _ _ _ _
Timetable	P _ _ _ _ _ _ _ _
List of questions	Q _ _ _ _ _ _ _ _ _ _ _ _ _
Not working	R _ _ _ _ _ _ _
Quiet	S _ _ _ _ _
Neat	T _ _ _
Below	U _ _ _ _
Musical Instrument	V _ _ _ _ _
Saturday/Sunday	W _ _ _ _ _ _
After five	_ _ X
Colour	Y _ _ _ _ _
Kind of line	Z _ _ Z _ _

READING

4 Education in England

Use the chart to complete the description.

3 4	Nursery
5 6 7 8 9 10 11	Primary
11 12 13 14 15 16	Secondary
16 17 18	Sixth Form College
18 19	University

Some children go to _____ school when they are _____ years old and stay there for _____ years. Nursery school is not compulsory - you don't have to go. Compulsory school starts at age with _____ school which lasts for years. When they are _____ children go to secondary school and stay there until they are _____. You can leave school then if you wish or go on to _____ for _____ years. People usually go to university when they are eighteen or nineteen.

UNIT 2 — LESSON 5

5 Conditional Sentences, Indefinite Pronouns, Rooms and Furniture, Compound Nouns, Listening.

GRAMMAR

1 Conditional Sentences Cause and Effect

Example feel tired

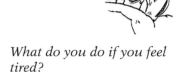

What do you do if you feel tired?
If I feel tired I have a rest.

Make questions and answers.

a feel hungry

_____

_____

b feel thirsty

_____

_____

c are cold

_____

_____

d are sad

_____

_____

e want to be alone

_____

_____

2 Indefinite Pronouns

Complete the sentences using these words.

anyone   anything   someone
something   everyone   everything
no-one   nothing

Example *(I think there's a problem.) Is **everything** all right?*

a (I think I'm alone.) _____ there?

b (I want to help. I don't mind what I do.)

Can I do _____ ?

c (All the people have gone.)

Where is _____ ?

d (I can see a person in the garden.)

There's _____ there.

e (Why am I the only person working?)

I can't do _____ .

f (I feel helpless.) I can't do

_____ .

g (I am not able to help.) I can do

_____ .

LESSON 5 UNIT 2

h (The garden is empty.)

_____

i (I'll do whatever you want.)

I'll do _____.

VOCABULARY

3 Put the words into columns.

armchair, bookshelf, chest of drawers, cooker, desk, dressing table, freezer, fridge, hi-fi, kettle, mattress, food mixer, sheet, sofa, wardrobe.

kitchen	bedroom	sitting room

4 Make new words by joining one word from each column.

Examples *arm + chair = armchair*
tooth + brush = toothbrush

air   brush   _____

arm   case   _____

bath   chair   _____

bed   hostess   _____

book   man   _____

business paper   _____

home   room   _____

news   room   _____

police   shine   _____

sun   table   _____

time   woman   _____

tooth   work   _____

LISTENING

5 Listen to the first part of Professor Black's talk.

Fill in the missing words.

There is no one _____ which is the best way to learn. _____ is different. _____ people learn best lying on the floor, listening to pop music. _____ people like to work at a desk in a _____ room. The important thing is to _____ out what is best for you. There are _____ useful techniques. If you find work boring, _____ stop because you will learn _____. Also the brain gets tired quite _____.

10

UNIT 2 | LESSON 6

Present Perfect, Present Simple and Present Continuous, Media Words, Symbols and Abbreviations, Grammar Words.

GRAMMAR

1 Present Perfect Tense + Just

Example *Adragon Eastwood De Mello **has just received** a bachelor's degree.*

You suggest things to your friend but he has always just done them! Write your friend's replies to your suggestions.

a Do you want something to eat?

b Let's go for a walk.

c How about some TV?

d Would you like a drink?

e Are you feeling tired?

f Let's go shopping.

g Would you like a game of tennis?

h Shall we go to the cinema?

2 Present Simple and Present Continuous

Answer the questions.

Example *What do you do when you're writing in English and don't know a word?*
I look it up in the dictionary.

a What are you doing now?

b How are you feeling?

c What do you wear to school/work?

d What clothes are you wearing now?

e Where do you come from?

f What do you do?

g Where do you sit when you're studying?

h How do you do? (careful!)

LESSON 6 **UNIT 2**

VOCABULARY

3 Put these words into columns. Some words go into both columns.

Article, advert, channel, crossword, daily, editorial, evening, front page, headline, interviewer, journalist, live, local, morning, the news, presenter, soap opera, weekly.

Newspapers	Radio/ TV

4 **Symbols and Abbreviations**

Match the symbols/abbreviations with their names.

Example *%   per cent*

adj _____

adv _____

BA _____

n _____

pl _____

sing _____

v _____

£ _____

1st _____

2nd _____

adverb, Bachelor of Arts, first, plural, pound, second, singular, verb, noun, adjective.

WORD PUZZLE

5 **Grammar Words**

Put the letters in the right order to make the words across. What is 1 Down?

Choose from: adjective, adverb, article, noun, plural, pronoun, simple, singular, tense, vocabulary.

Example *OSTINQUE = QUESTION*

a BRAVED
b GUNLAIRS
c VICEDJATE
d SENET
e PLIMSE
f NOONRUP
g UNNO
h CETRAIL
i LALRUP
j CLUBVARYOA

12

UNIT 3 LESSON 7

Simple Past, Present Simple Passive, Patterns, Clothes, Spelling.

GRAMMAR

1 Simple Past Irregular Verbs

Put the verbs in brackets into the simple past tense.

In 1990 Sandra _____ (sing) in a London pop group. She _____ (buy) her clothes cheaply and _____ (get) lots of bargains. Her jacket _____ (be) the most expensive item - it _____ (cost) £24. She _____ (think) 'What she Wants' _____ (be) wonderful and _____ (go) there often. In London Sandra _____ (drink) a lot of milk and _____ (eat) health food. She _____ (learn) how to play the guitar and _____ (make) friends easily. She _____ (give) singing lessons and _____ (go) to clubs at the weekend. She _____ (take) Italian lessons and _____ (write) to an Italian boyfriend.

2 Present Simple Passive

Example *Hair. The sides are shaved.*
Write sentences describing the pictures.

a close

b lock

c finish

d speak

LESSON 7 UNIT 3

VOCABULARY

3 Patterns

Match the words with the patterns.

Example  zig-zags

triangles   stripes   diamonds   checks
circles   squares   curves   rectangles
spots   diagonals

a 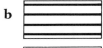 _____

b _____ _____

c _____ _____

d   _____

e  _____

f  _____

g  _____

h 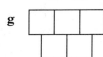 _____

i 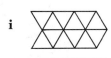 _____

j 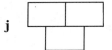 _____

4 Clothes

Find the odd one out.

Example *Jeans   Shorts   Pants   Socks*
Socks are worn on the feet.

a Skirt Blouse Tights Dress
b Gloves Sandals Trainers Boots
c Jacket T-Shirt Overcoat Duffle Coat
d Suit Trousers Pyjamas Jersey
e Tie Hat Scarf Belt

SPELLING

5 Find the words which have the same sound at the end but a different spelling.

Example *shoes   choose*

a bites _____

b blouse _____

c clothes _____

d coat _____

e scarf _____

f socks _____

g scissors _____

h hot _____

i these _____

j why _____

wrote, box, tights, trousers, chose, sees, what, allows, cough, trap, peas, laugh, lie, goes

UNIT 3   LESSON 8

8 Order of Adjectives, Past Simple Passive, Household Objects, The Natural World, Listening, Punctuation.

GRAMMAR

1 Order of Adjectives

Example *a bowl blue large*
a large blue bowl.

Put the words in the right order.

a an plate unusual octagonal

b a Japanese vase modern

c a bracelet Bedouin silver

d a small antelope wooden

e a ring gold 22 carat

f a television cheap Japanese

g a Swedish table white

h some huts round straw

i a suitcase leather black

j a book red cheap

2 Past Simple Passive

Imagine there was a storm on the island on the treasure map last night. Lots of things happened. Complete these sentences.

Example *The tall trees (blow down)*
The tall trees were blown down.

a The village (flood)

b The rocks (move)

c The straw huts (damage)

d The treasure (wash away)

e The Skeleton Coast (alter)

f The Silver Pool (empty)

LESSON 8 **UNIT 3**

VOCABULARY

3 Household Objects

Match the words on the left with those on the right to make the names of household objects. Use the pictures to help.

alarm	_____	board
clothes	_____	cleaner
ironing	_____	dryer
shower	_____	lamp
tin	_____	opener
bottle	_____	clock
hair	_____	curtain
kitchen	_____	hanger
table	_____	opener
vacuum	_____	sink

4 The Natural World

Fill in the missing words.

Treasure Island has two _____ and one _____. There are _____ in the centre and although there are no _____ there are lots of coconut trees. The island doesn't have any _____ although there is a lot of water. Equally there are no _____ although parts seem very hot and dry. The name of the _____ around the island is not known although the name of the northern _____ is.

LISTENING

5 Listen to the first part of the auction and fill in the missing words.

Good afternoon, ladies and gentlemen, and _____ to this afternoon's auction. We _____ with a group of items belonging to Colonel George _____ by his family from all over the _____. Item number 1 is a Turkish knife, _____ world war vintage, _____ back in 1917. This knife has a curved blade and a very _____ handle. I'd like to _____ the bidding, if I may please, at _____. Can I hear £20? £20, thank you very much sir. Any _____ on £20?

PUNCTUATION

6 Rewrite with capital letters and punctuation.

treasure the old man asked in surprise yes i replied ive got a map showing where it is where is it the old man asked im not telling you i answered im going to keep all the treasure for myself really exclaimed the old man then you dont know what the eighth clue is no i dont i said quickly the old man smiled back the eighth clue is that youll never find the treasure alone

16

UNIT 3 LESSON 9

Imperatives, *Will* Future, Money, Jobs, Spot the Difference.

GRAMMAR

1 Imperatives

Copy the headings below and put the sentences into the correct column.

Orders
Decide on the name of your auction
Requests
Can you pass the salt
Polite Requests
Would you mind opening the door

a Work in groups of four.
b Passports, please.
c I'd be grateful for some help.
d Could you possibly open the door?
e Make a note of what you paid.
f Please move along.
g I wonder if you could help me.
h Quiet please.
i Would you mind waiting a moment?
j Shut up.

2 *Will* Future

At the beginning of the auction the auctioneer gave these instructions. Complete using the *will* future.

All buyers _____ (go) to the cash desk at the end. They _____ (give) the number of the item they are buying to the cashier. The cashier _____ (ask) for the amount of money the buyer offered during the auction. The cashier _____ (give) the buyer a ticket with a number on it. The buyer _____ (return) to the auction room and collect the item.

VOCABULARY

3 Money

Underline the correct way of pronouncing these amounts of money.

Example £3.50 = *Three pounds fifty.*

a £14.00
  i Fourteen pounds
  ii Fourteen pound
  iii Fourteen hundred

b 50p
  i Fifty pence
  ii Half a pound
  iii Fifty pee

c £1.75
  i One hundred and seventy five
  ii One pound seventy five
  iii One hundred and seventy five pence

d £1500
  i Fifteen hundred pounds
  ii One and a half thousand pounds
  iii A thousand five

4 Jobs

An auctioneer sells things at an auction. What do these people do? Match the jobs with the things they work with. Then write a sentence describing the job.

Example *waiter/food*   *A waiter serves food.*

a baker   animals
b photographer   bread
c estate agent   cars
d greengrocer   food
e mechanic   letters
f porter   houses
g secretary   suitcases
h vet   photographer
i waiter   vegetables

17

LESSON 9   UNIT 3

a _____
b _____
c _____
d _____
e _____
f _____
g _____
h _____
i _____

Picture 1

5 Spot the difference

There are ten differences between the two pictures. Make ten sentences describing how picture 2 is different from picture 1.

Picture 2

1 _____
2 _____
3 _____
4 _____
5 _____
6 _____
7 _____
8 _____
9 _____
10 _____

UNIT 4 LESSON 10

10 Articles, Tenses, Leisure and Games, Theatre, Spelling, Word Puzzle.

GRAMMAR

1 Articles

Complete using *a*, *an*, or *the* where necessary. Sometimes no article is necessary.

Stockholm is (**a**) _____ capital city of (**b**) _____ Sweden. It's (**c**) _____ relaxing city full of (**d**) _____ lakes and (**e**) _____ parks. Many of (**f**) _____ inhabitants speak (**g**) _____ good English and visitors have (**h**) _____ wonderful time. Visit Grona Lund, (**i**) _____ oldest amusement park in Sweden, or try (**j**) _____ Vasa Museum where you can see (**k**) _____ very old ship. There are (**l**) _____ exciting boat trips to some of (**m**) _____ many islands around (**n**) _____ city. Or you can take (**o**) _____ ride in (**p**) _____ hot air balloon high in the sky over the city.

2 Tenses

Underline the correct tense.

There is a wonderful park in the centre of Stockholm. It *calls/is called* Kungsträdgården and the name *meant/means/mean* the King's Garden. There are cafés in the park where you *can find/are finding/found* every kind of food and drink you *wanted/have wanted/could want*. The stage in the park *will offer/offers/offered* nightly entertainment. Don't miss Kungsträdgården or you *miss/are missing/will miss* a marvellous experience.

VOCABULARY

3 Leisure and Games

Match these words with the definitions below. All the words are in Lesson **10**.

bowls, rapids, sauna, snooker, solarium.

a Finnish hot room. _____

b River running fast through rocks. _____

c Game played on grass with one small and several large balls. _____

d Game played indoors on a green table with small coloured balls. _____

e Place with artificial sun. _____

c B _____

d S _____

e S _____

f B _____

SPELLING

5 Complete.

Example *Shop   Shopping*

a	Dance	_____
b	Work	_____
c	Queue	_____
d	_____	Smoking
e	Feel	_____
f	_____	Thrilling
g	_____	Swimming
h	Train	_____

4 Theatre

Complete the labels of parts of a theatre with these words.

balcony   bar   box office   foyer   stage   stalls

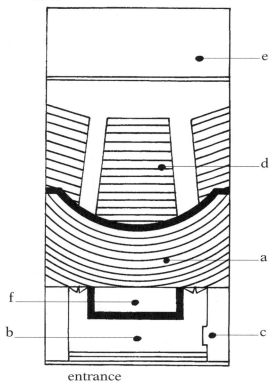

entrance

a B _____

b F _____

WORD PUZZLE

6 Find words in the text about London and the Holiday Village in Lesson **10** to complete the lines across. What is 1 Down?

There's an outside **a**

The museums are **b**

The **c** is in the picture 2.

The **d** are in the woodland.

The village is covered with a **e**

London has lots of **f** shops.

The boat trips are **g**

All the rooms have **h**

UNIT 4 — LESSON 11

11 Going to Future, Gerund, Sports Equipment, Defining, Prepositions, Listening.

GRAMMAR

1 Going to Future

Imagine you're at the Holiday Village. Look at the Information Board in Activity 5 in Lesson 11. Make sentences saying what you're going to do at these times.

10.00	At ten o'clock I'm going to play badminton.
11.00	_____
12.30	_____
14.00	_____
15.00	_____
16.00	_____
17.00	_____
18.00	_____
19.00	_____

2 Gerund

Example *I prefer lying under tropical trees.*

Complete.

a I really love _____ (swim) in the river.

b Jeff enjoyed _____ (wind-surf).

c I could watch tennis all day long but I hate _____ (play) it.

d Who prefers _____ (canoe) to _____ (cycle)?

e Would you mind _____ (look) after my clothes?

VOCABULARY

3 Sports Equipment

Label the equipment and say what sport it is used for.

Sports   Badminton Canoeing Golf
            Riding Sailing Table Tennis
            Tennis Volley-ball Wind-surfing

Equipment   Bat Board Clubs
                Life-jacket Net Paddles
                Racket Saddle

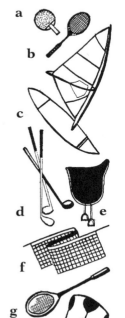

a _____
b _____
c _____
d _____
e _____
f _____
g _____
h _____
i _____

LESSON 11 **UNIT 4**

4 Defining

Example *What's a Jacuzzi? It's a kind of bath.*

Make and answer questions about these words. Use the help box where necessary.

a Sauna _____

b Pedaloe _____

c Aerobics _____

d Work out _____

e Turkish bath _____

Help Box
Individual exercise. Small hot room from Finland. Large hot room with steam. Cycle on water. Group exercise.

5 Prepositions

Fill in the missing prepositions.

about   to   with   up   out

a Nicky is going _____ holiday next week.

b Some people never stop talking _____ golf.

c He's learning _____ ride.

d She always has _____ win when she's playing tennis.

e He put _____ his tennis shoes and went _____ practise.

f How can you live _____ someone like that? He spends all day playing football.

g I waited by the swimming pool for hours but my friend didn't turn _____ so I went swimming alone.

h Please turn _____ the TV. I want to watch the European Athletics Championships.

i I can't find _____ where the jacuzzi is.

j Don't give _____ when you lose. You can't win all the time!

LISTENING

6 Listen to the first part of the interview with Nicky. Fill in the missing words.

INTERVIEWER Nicky, I believe you're going _____ the Sherwood Forest Holiday Village _____ your holiday this year. Why did you _____ it?

NICKY Well, a number _____ reasons, really. Firstly, a lot of _____ have recommended it quite _____, saying there are a lot of _____ to do for small children and as Joanna is now _____ months old we thought it would be a _____ place for us to go to where Jeff and I could enjoy ourselves and there'd be _____ to do for a young child.

UNIT 4 — LESSON 12

12 Question Formation, Adverbs, Food, Opposites, Word Puzzle, Spelling.

GRAMMAR

1 Question Formation

Write the questions.

Example *Where does curry from?*
Curry comes from India.

a What _____ ?
Chilli con carne contains meat, beans and chillies.

b How _____ ?
You make pizza from dough, cheese, and tomato.

c Who _____ ?
We all like hamburgers.

d When _____ ?
You drink port after an evening meal.

e Why _____ ?
The English like warm beer because they have a cold climate.

f Where _____ ?
Tea is grown in India, Sri Lanka and China.

g Why _____ ?
Some people call it *Coke* because it's easier to say than *Coca-Cola*.

h How _____ ?
You make tea by warming the pot, putting in tea and boiling water, and waiting for three minutes.

i Who _____ ?
The French invented Crêpes Suzettes.

j Where _____ ?
Sherry comes from Jerez in Spain.

2 Adverbs

Rewrite the sentences with these adverbs in the correct place.

never   always

Example *Spaghetti is boiled in water.*
Spaghetti is always boiled in water.

a Soup is the last course of the meal in Britain.

_____

b Fish and chips are served hot in England.

_____

c Soft drinks contain alcohol.

_____

d Green tea is drunk with milk.

_____

e Paella in Spain contains chicken and shell-fish.

_____

f Cheese fondue in Switzerland is made at the table.

_____

g Sweet and sour pork is served with rice or noodles in Chinese restaurants.

_____

LESSON 12 UNIT 4

VOCABULARY

3 Food

Complete using these words.

curry dessert goulash meat minced
onion pastry potato tomato

a Hamburgers are made of minced
m ———— and o ————.

b Bolognaise sauce can be made in many different ways, but usually contains
m ————, t ————, and o ————.

c Steak and kidney pie is covered with
p ————, and contains pieces of m ————, whereas Shepherds Pie is covered with
p ———— and contains m ———— meat.

d Both c ———— and g ———— contain hot spices.

e Ice-cream and cakes are examples of
d ————.

WORD PUZZLE

5 Use the pictures to help you complete the words across.
What does 1 Down spell?

4 Opposites

Fill in the word in column 2 which means the opposite of the word in column 1.

1	2
fresh	cold
hard	dry
hot	frozen
spicy	mild
strong	sliced
thick	soft
wet	thin
whole	weak

SPELLING

6 Find the food or drink in Lesson **12** which rhymes with these words.

Example Place   (fish)   Plaice

a Take   (meat)   ————
b Ham   (meat)   ————
c Hear   (Drink)   ————
d Taught   (Red sweet drink) ————
e Seize   (Made from milk)   ————
f Eye   (Food)   ————

UNIT 5 LESSON 13

13 This/That, These/Those, Used to, Make up, Listening, Prepositions.

GRAMMAR

1 This/That, These/Those

Example *Those dark brown eyes and that dark suit.*

Complete the sentences with *this, that, these* or *those*.

a Come over here and look at _____ waxwork.

Which one?

_____ one here.

b Can you see Boy George over there?

Yes. I think _____ boots look silly and _____ hat - it's ridiculous.

c Who's _____ between Boy George and Agatha Christie?

Do you mean the man with _____ checked trousers?

Yes. _____ 's the one.

Oh, I think _____ 's Picasso.

2 Used to

Example *My sister used to play with dolls.*

Make true sentences about your childhood using *used to* or *didn't use to*.

a Do homework all day

At weekends I

b Smoke a pipe

My father

c Drive a car

My mother

d Eating hamburgers

I

e Eating eggs

I

VOCABULARY

3 Make-up

Where do you use this make-up?

v mascara
ii face cream
iii lipstick
i nail varnish
iv hair spray

a hair
d cheeks
b eyelashes
e lips
c fingernails

LISTENING

4 Listen to the first part of the conversation between Pam and Judith. Fill in the missing words.

PAM Well, I recognise him, _____ you?

JUDITH No, who is it?

PAM That's JR.

JUDITH No, I _____ saw the televison programme.

PAM Yes, he's got _____ his smart suit.

JUDITH I don't think his hat goes _____ his suit. That sort of cowboy hat.

PAM Very smart suit and tie and belt.

JUDITH Um, he looks a bit _____ a menacing character though, _____ he?

PAM Yes, a bit frightening, and _____ the old man sitting on the chair?

JUDITH That's Picasso, _____ it?

PAM Oh is it? I didn't know he looked like _____ .

JUDITH Is he still alive?

PAM Don't think _____ .

PREPOSITIONS

5 Complete the conversation using these prepositions.

in on with at

Look _____ that figure over there - the one _____ the big hands.

The one _____ the checked jacket _____ ? Yes, that's him. Wasn't he _____ a TV series? He was a detective, wasn't he?

I'm not sure. I think it was _____ late _____ the evening so I didn't watch it.

_____ a bald head like that he's easy to remember.

Was he bald like that _____ the series or did he wear a wig when he was _____ TV?

No, like that! Really bald!

UNIT 5 **LESSON 14**

14 Question Tags, Question Formation, Adjectives, Compounds, Word Puzzle.

GRAMMAR

1 Question Tags
Asking for Agreement

Example *He looks a bit of a menacing character, doesn't he?*

The speaker wants you to agree with her. Finish these sentences in the correct way.

a Agatha Christie enjoyed laughing and joking, _____ ?

b Hitchcock's really short, _____ ?

c The visitors are always cheerful, _____ ?

d The collection was begun nearly 200 years ago, _____ ?

e Picasso was a really modern painter, _____ ?

f You'd like to meet JR, _____ ?

g Boy George's hair needs cutting, _____ ?

h Her murder stories are good, _____ ?

2 Question Formation

Turn these statements into questions.

Example *You were born in November.*
Were you born in November?

a She likes meeting and talking to people.
_____

b He's not happy at work.
_____

c She makes people laugh.
_____

d He used to be very rich.
_____

e She's been on TV a lot.
_____

f He's made a lot of films.
_____

g She helps other people.
_____

h He was born in March.
_____

i They both look happy.
_____

j You're Scorpio.
_____

VOCABULARY

3 Adjectives

Match the adjective in column 1 with its opposite in column 2.

1	2
bad-tempered	careless
boring	cruel
careful	dishonest
friendly	good-tempered
honest	impatient
kind	interesting
patient	weak

polite
powerful
thoughtful

rude
thoughtless
unfriendly

4 Compounds

Complete the sentences with compound adjectives. The example and first four are from Lesson 14.

Example *He works very hard.*
He is very hard-working

a She's full of confidence. She's

s_____ -c_____

b She's always getting angry. She's

b_____ -t_____ .

c He likes new ideas and listens to people.

He's o_____ -m_____ .

d She takes things calmly and doesn't get

upset. She's e_____ -g_____ .

e He is usually in a good mood and

doesn't get angry often. He's

g_____ -t_____ .

WORD PUZZLE

5 Use the pictures to help you complete the words across. The pictures show the first letter of the word. All the words are adjectives in Lesson 14. What is 1 Down?

Example *a musi©al*

UNIT 5 LESSON 15

15 Present Perfect, *Would like to*, Countries, Hobbies, Punctuation.

GRAMMAR

1 Present Perfect

Examples *I have never been to England.*
I have always lived in Belgium.
I have visited England once.

Write true sentences about yourself in the Present Perfect.

Example *(visit Paris)*
I have visited Paris twice.

a (visit New York)

_____

b (like spicy food)

_____

c (meet a TV star)

_____

d (live in the country)

_____

e (see Madonna)

_____

f (meet an American)

_____

g (hear the Stone Roses)

_____

2 Would like to

Read Lesson **15** again and complete the sentences using the correct form of the verb *like* or *would like to*.

Beatrix lives in Belgium. She _____ (work) for a local newspaper. She _____ (visit) India because she _____ (travel). She _____ (study) English and _____ (meet) some English people. Marie lives in France. She _____ (go) to the cinema and theatre. Marie _____ (write) to someone with similar interests. Both John and May _____ (swim). John _____ (make) European friends, while May _____ (make) friends from all over the world.

VOCABULARY

3 Countries

Label the map of Western Europe with the English names for the countries.

Example *Belgique = Belgium*

LESSON 15 UNIT 5

4 Hobbies

Find nine of the hobbies from Lesson **15** in this word square.

PUNCTUATION

5 Punctuate and lay out this letter as shown in Activity **4**, Lesson **15**.

bell college south road saffron walden essex cb113dp 5 october dear maria i have just arived at the college after a long journey everyone is so friendly and helpful that i feel at home already our classes today were great and im going to the disco tonight best wishes stefan

30

UNIT 6 LESSON 16

16 Passive, Adjectives, Face and Hands, Prepositions, Headlines.

GRAMMAR

1 Passive

Example *You cook the meat slowly.*
The meat is cooked slowly.

Put these instructions for cooking rice into the passive.

Cooking Rice

a You wash the rice with lots of water.

_____

b Then you add the rice to a saucepan of boiling water.

_____

c Next you cover the saucepan.

_____

d You then cook the rice for 8-11 minutes.

_____

e When there is no water left you take the rice off the heat.

_____

f You serve the rice immediately.

_____

VOCABULARY

2 Adjectives

Label the pictures using these words.

big fat long round sad short small smiling square thin

Use the lists in Activity **4b**, Lesson **16** to help.

Example   *Smiling*

a _____

b _____

c _____

d _____

e _____

f _____

g _____

h _____

i _____

3 Face and Hands

Label the pictures using these words.

cheek chin ear eyebrows forefinger
forehead knuckle nail palm thumb

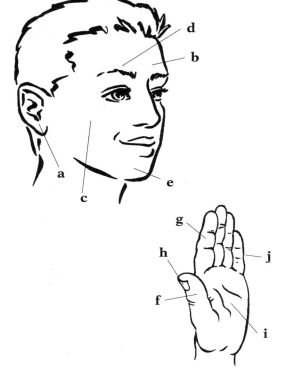

a _____
b _____
c _____
d _____
e _____
f _____
g _____
h _____
i _____
j _____

PREPOSITIONS

4 Fill in the missing prepositions.

in on out

To make a Hallowe'en pumpkin the first thing to do is to take _____ the inside. Then you cut holes _____ the pumpkin and make a funny face. A candle is put _____ the pumpkin and the lid is put _____ . Finally you put the pumpkin _____ the window.

READING

5 Match the newspaper headlines and the first lines of the stories.

a Football Violence ☐
b London Murder ☐
c Belgian Train Crash ☐
d Child Escapes Death ☐
e Russian American Meeting ☐

i In Helsinki today the President of the Soviet Union met the President of the United States.
ii In fighting outside the Leeds Football ground last night three people were injured.
iii A car crash in Manchester claimed the lives of three adults but a five year old girl was uninjured.
iv Police are seeking the killer of an eighteen year old youth after a fight in east London.
v Brussels police believe that two people were killed and six badly injured in a railway accident near the capital city today.

UNIT 6 — LESSON 17

17 Past Simple and Past Perfect, Linking Words, Animals, Adjectives, Listening, Spelling.

GRAMMAR

1 Past Simple and Past Perfect

Example *So, late one night, after everyone **had gone** to bed they **went** to the office.*

Put the verbs in brackets into the correct past tense.

Fay Merryweather's Story

'It _____ (be) a New York - Florida flight. We _____ (just) _____ (take off) and I _____ (go) to the galley at once. I _____ (look) in the oven door and _____ (see) a face. I _____ (go) to the flight deck. I _____ (tell) the flight engineer what I _____ (see). We _____ (go) back to the oven. The engineer _____ (look) at the face in surprise. He _____ (see) the face before!

2 Linking words

Example *In 1914 there was a story that an office in London was haunted. Two newspaper men decided to see if **this** was true.*

this refers to the story in the previous sentence.

What do the words in italics refer to in these sentences?

a 'I never walk under ladders. *It* brings bad luck.'

_____

b 'I know some people are afraid of black cats. I think *this* is silly.'

_____

c 'What do you think of *this*? I saw a UFO last night.'

_____

d 'My friend saw a ghost last night.' 'What did it look like?' *That's* the problem. She can't describe it.'

_____

e 'My brother is always reading ghost stories. *This* is why he never does his homework.'

_____

VOCABULARY

3 Parts of Animals

Label the parts of these animals.

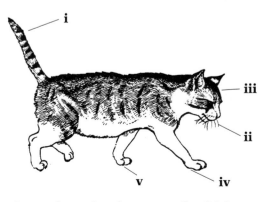

a   Cat   claws   head   paws   tail   whiskers

LESSON 17 **UNIT 6**

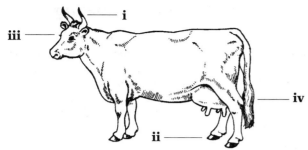

b Cow   head hooves (sing. hoof) horns tail

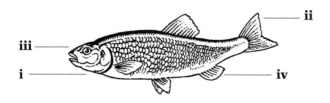

c Fish   fins gills head tail

I had this really strange experience _____ a plane some time ago. It was in 1973, _____ the Autumn. I was flying _____ New York to Florida in, er, an American Tri-Star Flight 318. Um, we had just taken _____ and I went to the kitchen galley to start preparing the meals _____ the 180 passengers _____ board.

4 Adjectives

Complete the sentences with the words in Activities **3b** and **c**, Lesson **17**.

a I wasn't frightened of the bird. I was _____ !

b Nothing happened for a long time so the men felt _____ .

c Little is the opposite of _____ .

d Gigantic and _____ mean much the same.

e Something which is extremely small is _____ .

LISTENING

5 Listen to the first part of Fay Merryweather's story. Fill in the missing words.

SPELLING

6 Silent Letters

Each of these words contains a 'silent' letter or letters which are not pronounced. Ring the letter or letters and write in a rhyme for the word from the box below.

Example g(h)ost   post

a midnight   _____
b wheel   _____
c caught   _____
d whisk   _____
e frighten   _____
f knife   _____
g through   _____
h high   _____
i lamb   _____

Word Box
flight fly heel jam lighten risk thought threw wife

UNIT 6 — LESSON 18

18 Linking Words, Past Simple, Food, Cooking, Reading, Punctuation.

GRAMMAR

1 Linking Words

These sentences describe how to mend a bicycle puncture. Put them in the right order, using the pictures to help you.

Mending a Bicycle Puncture

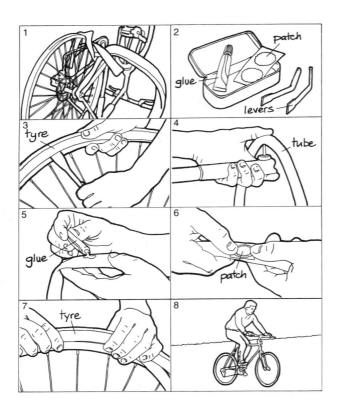

a First use the levers to take the tyre off the wheel. ☐
b When the glue is dry put on the patch. ☐
c Finally fill the tyre with air and cycle off. ☐
d When the tyre is off put some air in the tube and find the puncture. ☐
e Before you start to mend the puncture make sure you have everything you need. ☐
f Then you can put the tyre back on. ☐
g What you need is glue, a patch, and levers. ☐
h Next put glue on the puncture and wait a minute. ☐

2 Past Simple

Put the verbs into the correct column according to the way the end of the word is pronounced.

appeared bored closed covered decided
disappeared dropped haunted interested
locked looked mixed tossed worked

cooked	added	stirred

LESSON 18 — UNIT 6

VOCABULARY

3 Food

Write a sentence about each of these foods using the information in the boxes.

Foods   a Beef b Butter c Eggs
            d Flour e Lamb f Oil
            g Pepper h Sugar i Veal
            j Vinegar
Made From   Milk Wheat Vegetables
Comes From Calves Chickens Cows Sheep
Tastes   Hot Sharp Sweet

Example *Butter is made from milk.*

a _____
b _____
c _____
d _____
e _____
f _____
g _____
h _____
i _____
j _____

4 Cooking

Match the pictures to the words.

chopping board   knife   mixer
rolling pin   saucepan   scales   sieve
spoon   tin-opener   toaster

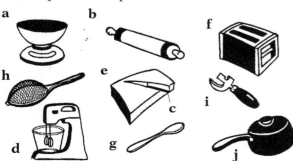

READING

5

There are ten 'extra' words in this recipe – words which do not belong. Find the words and underline them.

To make spaghetti bolognaise you cook need two large onions, a kilo of tomatoes, a kilo of minced meat, half a litre of water, garlic, oil, salt and pepper. You also bowl need a packet of spaghetti. First chop the whisk onions and tomatoes into small mixture pieces. Fry the onions and a little oven garlic in oil for three salt minutes. Add the tomatoes and cook for recipe two minutes. Then add water until the sauce pan is smooth. Bring to the boil and add the meat, salt and pepper. Stir hole well and cook for one hour. Boil heat the spaghetti in two litres of salted water until it is soft.

PUNCTUATION

6 Commas

Put in commas where necessary.

Making pancakes is always fun. You need a good frying pan and a high ceiling! The ingredients are eggs butter sugar flour and milk. Pancake Day is always a Tuesday and is popular with all the family. When I was a child we always ate pancakes with sugar and lemon but now people often eat them with jam and cream.
Pancake restaurants are popular all the year serving cheap quick meals of pancakes with fillings like cheese meat fish or vegetables.

36

UNIT 7 — LESSON 19

19 Questions, Present and Past Simple, Fruit and Vegetables, Definitions, Word Puzzle.

GRAMMAR

1 Questions

Example *How many meals do you eat a day?*

Make questions for these answers.

a How often _____ ?

I eat three times a day.

b How many times _____ ?

I usually eat fish twice a week.

c What _____ ?

Yesterday I had toast for breakfast, a sandwich for lunch, and fish for supper.

d How _____ ?

I'm afraid my diet isn't very healthy at all.

e How often _____ ?

I never eat chocolate.

f What _____ like _____ ?

Four years ago I was fat and overweight.

g What _____ ?

I like all kinds of food.

h What _____ ?

I liked cakes and fried foods.

2 Present Simple and Past Simple

Examples *She danced for at least three hours a day.*
I eat brown bread, fish, and lots of vegetables and salads.

Put the verbs in brackets into the correct tense.

a Esme _____ (smoke) and _____ (eat) snacks all the time.

b She _____ (feel) much better now she has changed her diet.

c I usually _____ (have) sandwiches for lunch when I was a student.

d High-calorie diets usually _____ (cause) health problems.

e I _____ (have) chips every day until I got so fat.

f Whenever I _____ (eat) chocolate I felt sick.

g Every time I exercise I _____ (get) hungry.

h She _____ (be) size 14 until she lost weight.

i Whenever I _____ (feel) hungry I have some fruit.

j When I was younger I always _____ (eat) crisps every evening.

LESSON 19 **UNIT 7**

VOCABULARY

3 Label the fruit and vegetables.

apple banana cabbage carrots cucumber grapes onion peas tomato orange

4 Potatoes

Potatoes can be cooked in many different ways. Match the kinds of potato with the definitions.

Potatoes	Ways of Cooking
a boiled	i baked in the oven unpeeled
b chips	ii boiled and puréed
c crisps	iii mashed and fried in balls
d croquette	iv cut into strips and fried
e jacket	v heated in water at 100°C
f mashed	vi peeled and baked in the oven in fat
g roast	vii boiled, sliced and fried
h sauté	viii sliced thin and fried

WORD PUZZLE

5 Complete the food words across. What is 1 Down?

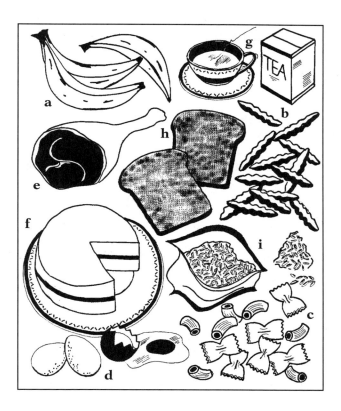

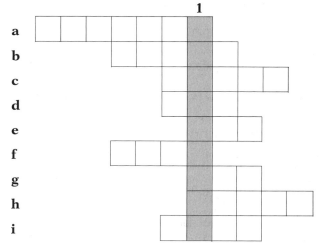

38

UNIT 7 LESSON 20

20 Past Continuous, Present Perfect, Athletics, Short Forms, Phrasal Verbs.

GRAMMAR

1 Past Continuous Tense

Example *Some competitors **were** still **running** at 6.30pm, nine hours after the race **started**.*

Put the verbs into the Past Simple or Past Continuous tense.

a Jenny Wood Allan _____ (still smile) when she finished the race.

b The competitors who _____ (run) for charity raised nearly £9,000,000.

c While most of the runners were serious about the marathon others said they ____ (only do) it for fun.

d 'I ____ (do) quite well,' said the man with the cake on his head, 'when it suddenly fell off!'

e 'I saw one of the competitors cheating,' said a spectator. 'He _____ (thumb) a car ride'.

f The man who _____ (play) the flute suddenly fell over.

g Some competitors were only just starting when Henryk Jorgensen ____ (finish) in 2 hours 10 minutes.

2 Present Perfect Tense

Example *I've proved my point. It wasn't easy and I broke down in tears at 22 miles.*

Put the verbs in brackets into the Present Perfect or Past Simple tense.

a 'I _____ (never run) so far in my life!'

b Over 2,000 women _____ (enter) the 1988 London Marathon.

c Radio News: 'The London Marathon is over and 21,000 of the 22,469 runners who _____ (start) _____ (finish).'

d TV news: 'I can see Ingrid Kristiansen, she's crossing the line, yes, Ingrid ____ (win) the women's marathon.'

e Richard Dolfe, 82, _____ (finish) the 1988 Marathon.

LESSON 20 **UNIT 7**

VOCABULARY

3 Athletics

Match the verbs with the pictures.

jog   jump   run   sprint   walk

4 Short Forms

Example *76 year-old granny Jenny Wood Allan*

To show friendliness family names are often shortened so *grandmother* becomes *granny*. Match these words with their short forms.

dad   mum   gran   mummy   granpa   nan   ma   papa

mother _____

father _____

grandmother _____

grandfather _____

PHRASAL VERBS

5 Complete the sentences with the correct phrasal verb.

break down =	start crying
break down =	stop working, eg a car
call off =	cancel
carry on =	continue
cut down on =	reduce
drop out =	leave (a competition)
egg on =	encourage
go off =	explode
go out =	stop burning
rake in =	collect money in large amounts

a Nearly £9,000,000 was _____ this year through charity competitors.

b The race was _____ at the last minute because of the heavy rain. It was impossible for the race to be run that day.

c The rain even made the Olympic flame _____ .

d I _____ in tears at 22 miles.

e The other runners were wonderful. They really _____ me _____ .

f James Newman ought to _____ eating.

g The gun _____ with a loud bang at the start of the race.

h Some of the competitors couldn't continue. They _____ part way through the marathon.

i One of the television cars following the race _____ . The competitors had to run around it.

j David Green _____ running even though he felt awful.

40

UNIT 7 — LESSON 21

Must, Past Participles, Rhymes, Reading, Punctuation..

VOCABULARY

1 Must

Example *Check with your Editor for the deadline when everything **must** be finished.*

Write sentences describing these road signs using *must* and *must not*.

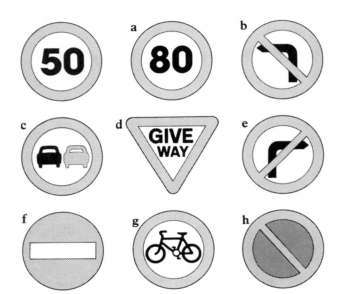

Example *50 sign = You must not drive faster than fifty kilometres an hour.*

a _____

b _____

c _____

d _____

e _____

f _____

g _____

h _____

i _____

2 Past Participles

Combine these sentences.

Example *You could use the information. It was collected in Lesson 19. = You could use the information collected in Lesson 19.*

a Find the picture. It is described on page 75.
b Use the interview with Mike Johnson. It is printed on page 41.
c Use the Pancake recipe. It was read in Lesson 18.
d Look at the definitions. They are included in Lesson 20.
e Check the results of the survey. It was done in Lesson 19.

LESSON 21 **UNIT 7**

VOCABULARY

3 Rhymes

Three words in each group rhyme. Underline the odd one out. Use your dictionary where necessary.

Example moon   june   spoon   <u>done</u>

    a wood   mood   food   rude
    b mud   mood   bud   blood
    c done   sun   bone   fun
    d ought   taught port   foot
    e word   stirred poured heard

READING

4 There are eight ideas for magazine articles in Lesson **21**, page **43**. Match the ideas with the headlines.

Ideas

a Class News
b School Diary
c Puzzles
d Eating and Exercise Survey
e Stories
f Songs/Poems
g Interview
h Food Tips

Headlines

i   Hot and Tasty
ii   **Mindbender**
iii *We're Fat and Lazy*
iv   **Terrified at Midnight**
v   *My Kind of Life*
vi   The Week
vii **Rock Me Now**
viii ***School Report***

PUNCTUATION

5 What are the names of punctuation marks in English? Match the names and marks.

apostrophe, brackets, colon, comma, exclamation mark, full stop, hyphen, inverted commas, semi-colon, question mark.

! _____

" _____

- _____

, _____

( ) _____

: _____

; _____

, _____

. _____

? _____

42

UNIT 8 LESSON 22

22 Superlatives, Gerund and Infinitive, Holidays, Compounds, Reading.

GRAMMAR

1 Superlatives

Example *the smallest house in Wales*

Look at the holiday brochure in Lesson 22.

Correct these sentences using the correct form of the adjectives below.

beautiful   big   exciting   good   old

a Conwy has the biggest house in Wales.

_____

b Colwyn Bay has the ugliest beach in Wales.

_____

c Caenarfon has one of the most modern castles in Wales.

_____

d Snowdonia is the worst place in Wales for activity holidays.

_____

e Portmeirion is the dullest village in Wales.

_____

2 Gerund and Infinitive

Fill in the gerund or infinitive of the verbs in brackets after *forget* and *remember*.

Examples *I remember visiting Caernarfon Castle. 1 visit 2 remember*
Remember to visit Caernarfon Castle. = 1 remember   2 visit

a When we went camping in North Wales I forgot _____ (take) the food.

b Remember _____ (pack) good shoes when you go walking in Scotland.

c Do you remember _____ (swim) at Colwyn Bay?

d I remember _____ (get) sun-burnt when on holiday in Cornwall.

e Don't forget _____ (take) your camera when we go to Snowdonia.

VOCABULARY

3 Holidays

Correct the spelling of these holiday activities.

a Waking in Scotland

_____

b Windesurfing

_____

c Sunbathing on the beech in Cornwall

_____

LESSON 22 **UNIT 8**

d Canoing in Snowdonia

e Climing in the Lake District

f Birdwashing on Anglesey

g Going on a minitur railway

4 Compounds

Make new sentences using compound words.

Example The *village looks Italian* = *It's an Italian-looking village.*

a This rose smells sweet.

It's ─────

b The name sounds German.

It's ─────

c The woman looks important.

It's ─────

d The game moves fast.

It's ─────

e This curry tastes strong.

It's ─────

READING

5 Read the passage and then answer the questions, True (T) or False (F).

Athens City Guide

Introduction
The city of Athens is over 4,000 years old. Today the capital of Greece is a busy modern city with a population of over two million. Athens is both an important commercial centre and a popular destination for tourists.

Your Arrival in Athens
Hellenikon Airport is 9 miles (14 kilometres) from the city. At the airport there are banks, cafés, restaurants and shops. Buses and taxis run to the centre.

Hotels
Athens has many excellent hotels and it is a good idea to book ahead, particularly during the busy summer tourist season.

Restaurants
All the leading hotels have first class restaurants, some with dancing in the evenings. But for the authentic life of Athens try one of the many 'tavernas' in the Plaka district below the Acropolis. Taste some of the wonderful specialities like Souvlaki (grilled pieces of meat), Tsatsiki (cucumber, yoghourt and garlic), or Moussaka (minced meat and aubergine or potato covered with a cheese sauce).

Excursions
Morning and afternoon coach tours, with multi-lingual guides, depart at 9am from Constitution Square.

Climate and Clothing
Athens has a wonderful climate and lots of sunny days. Spring and autumn are ideal for visiting Greece. The nights in summer are reasonably cool and in winter temperatures rarely fall below nine degrees.

True or False?

a The airport is nine kilometres from the city centre. ☐

b The best hotels are in the Plaka district. ☐

c You can get a sight-seeing tour from Constitution Square. ☐

d It often snows in Athens during the winter when temperatures rarely reach nine degrees. ☐

e There are many hotels in Athens. ☐

f Tsatsiki contains meat. ☐

44

UNIT 8 — LESSON 23

23 Past Simple Irregular Verbs, Passive, First Aid, Listening, Word Puzzle.

GRAMMAR

1 Past Simple, Irregular Verbs

Fill in the correct verb in the Past Simple tense.

get go have say see take tell think

Ian, Joyce and Pete all _____ holidays in North Wales. They _____ the interviewer about their holidays. Ian _____ to Portmeirion. Both Joyce and Pete _____ that they had been to Snowdonia. Ian _____ that Portmeirion was expensive. Joyce _____ the train up Snowdon but she _____ very little because of the mist. Peter only _____ part way up Snowdon because of the ice.

2 Passive

Example *We strongly recommend a hot drink = A hot drink is strongly recommended.*

Change these sentences in the same way.

a You really need good boots.

_____

b We highly recommend the Portmeirion Hotel.

_____

c We definitely advise taking plenty of warm clothing.

_____

d We don't advise wearing jeans.

_____

e We don't permit camping.

_____

VOCABULARY

3 First Aid

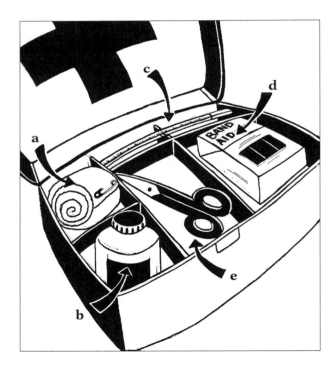

Label the contents of this first aid kit.

aspirin   scissors
bandage   thermometer
plaster

LESSON 23 UNIT 8

LISTENING

4 Listen to the interview with Ian and fill in the missing words.

INTERVIEWER Ian, when you visited North Wales was there anything _____ that you did?

IAN Um, yeah, I did one thing that I _____ enjoyed. I visited this place called Portmeirion which I've _____ wanted to go to. . . and that was really _____ .

INTERVIEWER Can you tell me about it?

IAN Well, there's a hotel which is _____ incredible as well to look at, but it's far too _____, so I didn't stay there. I just walked around the village and had a look at it, and there's a very _____ pottery there called the Portmeirion pottery.

INTERVIEWER Do you think I should go?

IAN Oh _____ and take lots of money with you.

WORD PUZZLE

5 Use the clues to fill in the words across. The words are to do with hill-walking. What is 1 Down?

Clues

a You blow it
b On your head
c To see at night
d In case you're hungry
e To warm you up
f To find your way
g To keep you warm
h On your feet
i On your hands
j In case of an accident
k Lunch

46

UNIT 8 LESSON 24

24 Word Order, *Should*, Towns, Dates, Prepositions.

GRAMMAR

1 Word Order

Put the words in the right order to make sentences. You may need to add punctuation. The first word of each sentence is underlined.

Example *In six weeks' time the prize is a new book which will be in the shops about our town.*
The prize is a new book about our town which will be in the shops in six weeks' time.

a with its marvellous shopping York is nearly two thousand years old and has something for everyone and excellent restaurants

b with a long history a friendly place an attractive town near Cambridge Saffron Walden is

c in South America and covering an area of 60 square miles with over 4 million inhabitants Rio is one of the largest cities

d is built on 14 islands the capital of the old kingdom of Sweden Stockholm on the Baltic Sea coast

e the second largest city beautifully situated on the Rhine Basel is with a population of 223,000

2 Should

Rewrite these sentences using *should*.

Example *The idea is that the poster is for the general tourist.*
The poster ought to be for the general tourist =
*The poster **should** be for the general tourist.*

a The idea is that the poster gives general information.

b Your group ought to contain no more than four people.

c The poster ought to make our town look interesting.

d The winning poster is meant to attract tourists.

e The idea is that you decide which tourist attractions to use.

VOCABULARY

3 Towns

Complete the sentences with words from the list.

art galleries   botanical gardens   church
market   museum   park   pubs   youth hostel

a The _____ in Cambridge contain a wide variety of different plants and trees.

b _____ are typically English and now often serve good food as well as drinks.

c Staying at a _____ is a very cheap way of travelling and is not limited to young people.

d You can play tennis or football in the _____ and there is a children's playground as well.

e The _____ in Saffron Walden has an excellent collection of objects from the town's past.

f In Cambridge there are a number of _____ which display the work of local painters.

g Cambridge _____, in the centre of town, is a good place to buy fresh vegetables and old clothes.

4 Dates

Example Between 1300 and 1399 = fourteenth century.

Below are some famous dates. Complete the sentences with the correct century.

1066   1492   1876   1968   2001

a Columbus discovered America in the _____ century.

b Arthur C Clarke's famous book takes place in the _____ century.

c The French invaded England in the _____ century.

d The first man landed on the moon in the _____ century.

e Bell invented the telephone in the _____ century.

PREPOSITIONS

5 Fill in the correct prepositions.
by   for   in   of   on   over   to   with

There is something _____ everyone _____ York, which has _____ 1900 years of history. Walking _____ the old town wall and _____ the river are popular _____ tourists. The National Railway Museum is one of the best _____ the world. You can spend your time shopping _____ the old narrow streets _____ the town, or go _____ the Jorvik Viking Centre.

UNIT 9 LESSON 25

25 Questions, Possessives, Radio, Numbers, Reading.

GRAMMAR

1 Questions   Present Simple

Look at the programme guide to Radio Four in Activity 4, Lesson 25. Write questions for these answers.

Example *When does The Today Programme start?*
It starts at 6.30.

a _____
It can take four hours.

b _____
Dame Edna Everage does.

c _____
It's called 'Dolly's Mother'.

d _____
It's about the Secret Service.

e _____
It finishes at 12.25.

f _____
The News is on four times.

g _____
It's about vegetarianism.

2 More Questions

Look at the programmes listed in Activity 2, Lesson 25. Complete these questions.

a When _____ on?
It's at ten thirty.

b What _____?
It's called 'I wish I had a Parrot'.

c What _____ about?
Holidays.

d When _____ on?
Half past four.

e What _____ about?
Politics.

f When _____ on?
Twenty five past six.

VOCABULARY

3 Possessives

Example You and Yours

Complete.

a Me and _____

b She and _____

c They and _____

d We and _____

e He and _____

4 Radio Programmes

Look at the types of programmes in the questionnaire in Activity **1**, Question **3**, Lesson **25**. What types are these programmes?

Example *Beethoven Concert*
               Classical music

a What's the Answer?

_____

b Rain or Sunshine?

_____

c Terror at Midnight

_____

d Laugh a Minute

_____

e The Top Twenty

_____

ii	third	four	x	fifth	nine
ix	ninth	ten	iii	second	eight
v	seventh	two	viii	tenth	seven
vii	eighth	five	iv	fourth	three

READING

6 TV Programme Guide

At what time can you watch the following programmes?

5.35	Neighbours.
6.00	Six o'clock news. Weather.
6.30	Look East. Local news.
7.00	Quiz. Big Prizes!
7.30	Eastenders. Family Life in London.
8.00	May to December. Old Husband, Younger Wife.
8.30	Question of Sport. Sporting Quiz.
9.00	Nine o'clock news. Weather.
9.30	Paradise Club. Night Club Excitement.
10.20	Film 91. The Latest Films.
10.50	Thriller: Private Detective.
12.10	Weather.

5 Numbers

Match the numbers from the box below.

Example *1 = one = i = first*

10 _____

2 _____

4 _____

7 _____

9 _____

3 _____

5 _____

8 _____

a The news

_____

b A quiz

_____

c The weather

_____

d A cinema programme

_____

e A police programme

_____

UNIT 9 LESSON 26

26 Question Formation, Passive, Space, Measurements, Prepositions of Time.

GRAMMAR

1 Question Formation

Danny Weaver is questioned by the police after his arrest. Below are the police inspector's notes.

Saturday pm	Weaver visited museum.
17.00	Hid in small room next to Main Exhibition.
24.00	Got out tools, began work.
Sunday	Cut Siren Goddess from case.
	Put copy in case.
	Hid again.
Monday	
10.00	Leave hiding place, join visitors.
10.30	Leave museum.

Complete the inspector's questions.

a Where _____ you go on Saturday afternoon?

b Where _____ at closing time?

c When _____ work?

d What _____ Sunday?

e How _____ leave the museum on Monday?

2 Passive

Put the sentences below into the passive.

Example *A thief stole the statue from the museum.*
The statue was stolen from the museum.

a Rawlings told the story in the departure lounge.

The story _____

b The thief cut the statue from its case.

The statue _____

c The reporter interviewed Rawlings on his return to Earth.

Rawlings _____

d Radio Earth interviewed Danny Weaver by satellite radio.

Danny Weaver _____

e They gave Danny a special job to do.

Danny _____

VOCABULARY

3 Space

Label the picture with these words.

moon   rocket   satellite   space shuttle   stars

51

4 Measurements

Example *statue/8 inches/high*
The statue is about twenty centimetres high.

Make complete sentences from the details below. Use the conversion table, and a calculator if necessary.

> **Conversion Table** *A Quick Rough Method*
> - To convert inches into centimetres multiply by two and a half. So eight inches is about twenty centimetres.
> - To convert feet into metres multiply by three and divide by ten.
> - To convert miles into kilometres add three fifths of the number of miles.
> - To convert yards into metres subtract one tenth.

a Detective Inspector Rawlings/6 feet/tall

_____

b Mount Everest/29,028 feet/high

_____

c speed limit/30 miles an hour

_____

d distance/100 yards

_____

e book/3 inches/thick

_____

5 Prepositions of Time

Fill in the correct prepositions.

as   at   by   for   from   in   on   since

> The story of the discovery of the Siren Goddess is an interesting one. _____ two thirty _____ the afternoon _____ December 25th, 2020 a rocket from Earth landed on Mars. It had been travelling _____ weeks and the crew were tired. Mr Siren, the pilot, made a mistake on landing and crashed the rocket. No-one was hurt but the rocket engine was damaged and they couldn't take off again. 'Don't worry,' said the pilot, 'someone will come and rescue us _____ a few hours.' The crew waited _____ days for help but no-one came. _____ then there was no food left, so they decided to leave the rocket. The rocket was in a hole in the ground and as he was getting out Siren saw something sticking out of the ground. He picked it up. It was a small stone statue. As he picked the statue up something strange happened: the rocket engine started! Siren got back in and took off. _____ then on Siren kept the little statue in his rocket. 'It's magic,' he used to say, 'it's my goddess!' Siren flew safely all around space _____ years with the Siren Goddess, and when he died he left it to the Meridian Museum, where it has been ever _____ .

UNIT 9 LESSON 27

27 Question Formation, Present Perfect or Past Simple? Leaders, *Say* and *Tell*, Reading.

GRAMMAR

1 Question Formation Present Perfect Tense

Write the questions.

Example *(meet famous people)*
Have you met any famous people?

a (hear the news)

_____

b (see the producer)

_____

c (decide on the announcer)

_____

d (prepare your news items)

_____

e (record your programme)

_____

2 Present Perfect or Past Simple?

Put the verbs in brackets into the correct tense.

'Good evening, here are the news headlines. The Prime Minister _____ (announce) a cut in interest rates to fourteen per cent. There _____ (be) a severe accident on the A11 near Stumps Cross and police _____ (close) the road. Football, and Cambridge United _____ (beat) Leeds in the Cup. Finally, the weather _____ (be) a warm dry day in most parts of the region and we can expect this to continue for the rest of the week.

And now the news in detail. A short time ago, the Prime Minister, speaking in Downing Street, _____ (say) that interest rates would fall to fourteen per cent on Monday. Here's our financial correspondent with comment from the City . . . Earlier today police _____ (close) the A11 near Stumps Cross after a severe accident involving a car and a lorry. A drum of acid _____ (fall) off the back of the lorry, hitting the car. Three people were taken to Addenbrooke's Hospital where a spokesman _____ (say) that they were 'poorly'. Football, and Cambridge United are through to the next round of the Cup after they _____ (beat) Leeds one nil this afternoon. Here's our sports correspondent . . . '.

LESSON 27 UNIT 9

VOCABULARY

3 Leaders

The producer is the person who is in charge of a radio programme. Name the person in charge of the following. Choose from this list.

captain   chef   editor
headmaster/mistress   manager
Prime Minister

a newspaper _____

b school _____

c The British Government _____

d hotel _____

e ship _____

f kitchen _____

g football team _____

h bank _____

4 Say and Tell

Complete the sentences with the correct form of the verb *say* or *tell*.

a Can you _____ me the time please?

b The producer will _____ you what to do.

c Please _____ that again.

d The announcer _____ a joke at the end of the programme.

e She _____ that the governement had resigned.

f How do you _____ 'announcer' in your language?

g Rawlings _____ the story of the Siren Goddess.

h Please _____ me when you are ready.

i What did you _____ ? I'm sorry I couldn't hear you.

j I don't think Mr Maccar is _____ the truth.

READING

5 This is an article from a local newspaper. The first paragraph is correct but the other paragraphs are in the wrong order. Put the paragraphs in the correct order.

Down Your Road
This Week: Histon Road

a   Histon Road has slowly grown over the last two hundred years. For a long time it was just a narrow track leading to the village of Histon. [1]

b   Finally in the 1920s the town council built a large number of houses on the road. A pleasant park was opened at the same time. ☐

c   Major development came in the middle of the last century when houses were built on both sides of the road. ☐

d   Early last century it was still largely farmland. Farmers grew food for the local market. ☐

e   Today it is a busy road with plenty of traffic and life. It has excellent shopping and facilities. ☐

f   First there were just a few small houses and a farm. ☐

g   Then, in about 1870, more houses were built further towards Histon and shops were developed. ☐

54

UNIT 10 — LESSON 28

28 Indirect Speech, Animals, Groups, Word Puzzle.

GRAMMAR

1 Indirect Speech

Example *'There are two clues in this case,' said Holmes, 'a hat and a goose.'*
Holmes said that there were two clues, a hat and a goose.

Put these sentences into indirect speech.

a 'Why don't you visit my flat?' Madeleine asked Paul.

b 'Why are you seeing Sylvie?' Madeleine asked Paul.

c 'Something's wrong,' Mary said.

d 'Why is Max so afraid?' Frederick asked.

e 'I hate Henry Blake,' said Clara.

f 'Drugs kill thousands of people every year,' Kay said.

g 'The record company want us to make our first record,' Tony said.

h 'I don't want to go to the opera festival in Salzburg,' said Sam.

i 'I want to travel on my own,' said Sam.

2 Indirect Speech

Put these sentences into indirect speech.

Example *'I'll go far away to another country,' Clara dreamt.*
Clara dreamt she would go far away to another country.

a 'Everything's going to be wonderful,' Clara thought.

b 'We're going to get married,' Madeleine thought.

c 'We'll try and help Max,' said Beatriz.

d 'I'm going to expose the world of drugs,' said Kay.

e 'We're going to make a record!' Tony told the band.

f 'I'll spend the summer in Sardinia,' Sam told her parents.

VOCABULARY

3 Animals

A young goose is called a gosling. Find the picture and name these young animals.

kitten   calf   foal   puppy   lamb

4 Groups

A group of geese is called a gaggle. Match the groups of people, things or animals to the word that describes them.

audience   cards
bunch   cows
flock   keys
herd   people in the cinema/theatre
pack   sheep

WORD PUZZLE

5 Anagrams

Anagrams are puzzles where the letters of a word are mixed up. For example, ANABAN is an anagram of BANANA.

Solve the anagrams of these words which describe kinds of stories.

a LELTRHIR ☐☐☐☐☐☐☐
b RORORH   ☐☐☐☐☐☐
c LAFYIM   ☐☐☐☐☐☐
d FLEARILE ☐☐☐☐ ☐☐☐☐
e MLANIA   ☐☐☐☐☐☐
f DEMOCY   ☐☐☐☐☐☐
g VICTEEDET ☐☐☐☐☐☐☐☐

UNIT 10 LESSON 29

29 Passive, Articles, Compound Nouns, Noises, Phrasal Verbs, Reading.

GRAMMAR

1 Passive

Example Hat Found Peterson
The hat was found by Peterson.

Here are more of Sherlock Holmes's notes. Expand the notes into full sentences.

a *Goose Also Found Peterson*

b *Tall Man Attacked Group Rough Young Men*

c *Shop Window Broken Stick*

d *Label Tied Goose's Leg*

e *Jewel Found Inside Goose*

f *Blue Carbuncle Stolen Hotel Cosmopolitan*

g *Robbery Discovered James Ryder Assistant Manager*

h *Jewel Kept Desk Bedroom*

2 Articles

Example *It isn't a diamond. It's the Blue Carbuncle.*

Fill the spaces with *a*, *an* or *the* where necessary.

_____ story of _____ Blue Carbuncle is one of Sherlock Holmes's best. _____ theft of _____ diamond from _____ hotel bedroom at _____ Christmas puzzled everyone. Holmes's first clues were _____ hat and _____ goose. Holmes and Dr Watson went to Covent Garden Market and heard _____ argument. _____ man who was arguing tried to run away but Holmes caught him.

VOCABULARY

3 Compound Nouns

Examples *Jewel-box (with -)*
shop window (without -)

Make compound nouns by choosing one word from each column.

Christmas	bedroom
dining	cutting
hotel	dinner
language	laboratory

57

language	manager
market	place
newspaper	room
sitting	school
under	story

4 Noises

Complete the sentences with the correct form of the words from this list.

bang cough crash scream sneeze snore

a He had a bad cold and kept on _____ .

b She smoked too much and _____ a lot.

c The broken glass made a loud _____ .

d The gun made a big _____ .

e At Halloween you often hear _____ .

f People tell me that I _____ at night so they don't want to share a room with me.

PHRASAL VERBS

5 **Example** *Someone had broken into the Countess's room.*

Complete these sentences using these words.

after away back out round

a The group of rough young men ran _____ . (= escape)

b Don't come _____ here again. (= return)

c Holmes and I ran _____ the man. (= chase)

d The man sprang _____ . (= turn quickly)

e Did you find _____ what happened to the Blue Carbuncle? (= discover)

READING

6 Match the story titles with the descriptions. Put the letter of the description in the boxes.

Titles	
Dear Jan Love Ruth	☐
Frankenstein	☐
Murder at Mortlock Hall	☐
One Pair of Eyes	☐
Rich Man Poor Man	☐
Stars For A Day	☐
The Boy Who Was Afraid	☐

Descriptions

a Belinda Smart does not want to spend her holidays in the country with her blind cousin Tim, but events make her change her mind.
b Everybody hated Trevor Marshall, but which of his enemies killed him?
c A surprise money order makes Adam rich . . . . Until he comes up against the problems of cashing it.
d A tragic love affair between an English girl and a Polish student.
e Two stories of unexpected fame and fortune.
f One of the most famous horror stories ever written.
g Mafatu, a Polynesian boy, faces the sea, his biggest fear.

UNIT 10 — LESSON 30

30 Question Formation, Linking Words, *Do* and *Make*, Education, Spelling.

GRAMMAR

1 Question Formation

Example *Frederick is from Switzerland.*
Where's Frederick from?

Make questions using these words.

what   where   who   why

a _____
Frederick is studying at Cromwell College.

b _____
It's a language school.

c _____
Beatriz is also a student.

d _____
It's called 'The Last Recording'.

e _____
He's from Switzerland.

f _____
Because he wanted to learn English.

g _____
He unpacked and then went for a walk.

2 Linking Words

Put the sentences below in the right order and put the verbs in brackets in the past simple or past perfect tense. Write out the story.

a It _____ (be) a friend of his who _____ (die) the year before.

b She _____ (see) a man's face in the door.

c When she _____ (get) to the flight deck she _____ (speak) to the engineer.

d This _____ (be) what really _____ (happen) to a stewardess on a flight from New York to Florida.

e As the engineer _____ (look) the face _____ (say) 'Fire'!

f The stewardess and engineer _____ (return) to the galley.

g After they _____ (take) off she _____ (go) to the galley to warm up the meal.

h This time the engineer _____ (recognise) the face.

i She _____ (run) out of the galley and up to the flight deck.

j Just as they _____ (approach) the oven the face _____ (appear) again.

k Just as she _____ (open) the door she _____ (have) a terrible shock.

59

VOCABULARY

3 *Do* and *Make*

Fill in the correct form of *do* or *make*.

a Frederick had to _____ his homework every night at Cromwell College.

b He also had to _____ his bed every morning!

c He had to _____ his own washing but not the washing up.

d There weren't many rules at the College but an important one was that it was forbidden to _____ a noise after 11.30.

e Frederick was _____ an English Language course.

f If he _____ well on the course he would pass his examinations.

g Frederick _____ lots of friends at the College.

h He was good at English and didn't _____ many mistakes.

i He _____ his best in class and _____ lots of notes.

j One day he _____ a complaint about the strange noises in the language laboratory.

4 Education

Use the clues below to fill in the words across. What is 1 Down?

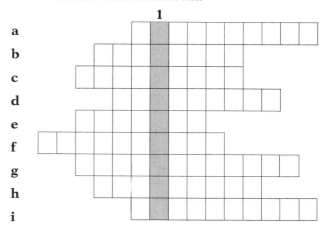

i Male person in charge of a school.
ii People who study.
iii IBM make them.
iv School for 11-18 year olds.
v First school.
vi You learn science or languages in one.
vii You take these every year and need to pass them!
viii Usually made on a cassette.
ix Where you study for a degree.

SPELLING

5

Put the words into the correct column according to their final sound.

approach   baggage   beach   college
cottage   edge   fetch   judge   language
reach   teach   which

Bridge	**Rich**
language	which
_____	_____
_____	_____
_____	_____
_____	_____
_____	_____

Key

UNIT 1

Lesson 1

1 a What colour is the blind?
   b What shape is the table?
   c What size is the rug?
   d What colour is the bookcase?
   e What shape is the room?
   f What size is the box?

2 got bought is echoes is did not look got cleaned look
   is keep bought had is like

3 a Ankara - Turkey - Turkish
   b Athens - Greece - Greek
   c Beijing - China - Chinese
   d Brasilia - Brazil - Portuguese
   e Buenos Aires - Argentina - Spanish
   f Cairo - Egypt - Egyptian
   g Copenhagen - Denmark - Danish
   h Madrid - Spain - Spanish
   i Moscow - Russia - Russian
   j Paris - France - French
   k Rome - Italy - Italian

4 bathroom - sink, toilet
   bedroom - wardrobe
   dining room - table
   kitchen - cooker
   living room - sofa, desk, bookcase

5 INTERVIEWER: What do you use it for?
   CORRINNE: It's a music cupboard actually.
   INTERVIEWER: Is it English?
   CORRINNE: No, Greek.
   INTERVIEWER: Do you like Greek things?
   CORRINNE: Very much. The rug is Greek, too.
   INTERVIEWER: How about the futon?
   CORRINNE: That's Japanese of course.
   INTERVIEWER: Why do you like red?
   CORRINNE: Because it's a warm colour, I suppose. Why are you asking me all these questions?
   INTERVIEWER: I don't know. I'm just curious.

6 in favourite here warm lights which cosy for up again the just from got ago

Lesson 2

1 gets goes check is is gets has goes buys goes

2 have am working am seeing is does not work is coming is visiting works is is arriving

3 11am   coffee   Good morning
   1pm   lunch   Good afternoon
   4pm   tea   Good afternoon
   7.30   dinner   Good evening
   11pm   cocoa   Good night

4 1 neck   2 wrist   3 thumb   4 heel
   5 toe   6 ankle   7 knee   8 finger
   9 thigh 10 elbow

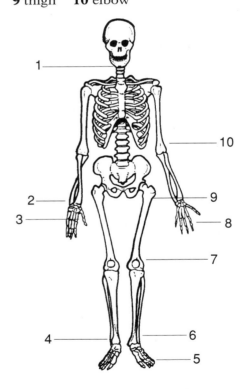

5 at past in for at past at to at past for at to to from to in in at in

Lesson 3

1 a highest/higher
   b smallest/larger

Key

    c longest/longest/longer
    d larger/largest
    e biggest/smaller/faster

2   **a** Have you heard her?
    b Have you tried it?
    c Have you visited it?
    d Have you seen it?
    e Have you read it?

3   **a** courts
    b pools
    c courses
    d gymnasium
    e ring
    f pitch

4   **a** husband
    b sister
    c uncle
    d aunt
    e mother
    f cousin
    g grandmother and grandfather

5   **Description**

Mario is twenty and comes from Turin in northern Italy. He was born on the first of January and each year has a combined birthday and New Year party. Mario's friends say he has a good sense of humour.

Likes

He likes discos, hamburgers and Alpha Romeo cars.

Hobbies

Mario speaks English and German as well as Italian, and has visited most European countries. His favourite sport is volleyball. He plays the guitar and his favourite group are Roxette, who come from Sweden.

Family

He has two brothers, Attilio and Luigi.

Work

Mario is a student at Rome University. He is studying engineering and wants to work for Fiat.

UNIT 2

Lesson 4

1   likes would like would like likes like
would not like
would like to like likes would like

2   best most expensive more useful best
best worst
more thoughtful most least best
more important

3   answer breakfast coffee dictionary
evening friends Greece
homework interesting Japan knee
Library Monday night opinion
programme questionnaire relaxing
silent tidy under violin weekend
six yellow zig-zag

4   nursery three two five primary
seven eleven sixteen
6th Form College two

Lesson 5

1   **a** What do you do if you feel hungry?
       If I feel hungry I eat something.
    b What do you do if you feel thirsty?
       If I feel thirsty I have a drink.
    c What do you do if you are cold?
       If I am cold I put on a sweater.
    d What do you do if you are sad?
       If I am sad I talk to a friend.
    e What do you do if you want to be alone?
       If I want to be alone I go to my room.

2   **a** Is anyone there?
    b Can I do anything?
    c Where is everyone?
    d There's someone there.
    e I can't do everything.
    f I can't do anything.
    g I can do nothing.
    h There's no-one there.
    i I'll do everything.

3

Kitchen	Bedroom	Sitting-room
freezer	chest of drawers	armchair
fridge	dressing table	bookshelf
kettle	sheet	desk
mixer	mattress	hi-fi
cooker	wardrobe	sofa

Key

4 airhostess, armchair, bathroom, bedroom, bookcase, businessman/woman, homework, newspaper, policeman/woman, sunshine, timetable, toothbrush.

5 way everyone some other quiet find some then nothing quickly

Lesson 6

1
- **a** I've just eaten.
- **b** I've just been for a walk.
- **c** I've just watched TV.
- **d** I've just had a drink.
- **e** I've just had a rest.
- **f** I've just been shopping.
- **g** I've just played tennis.
- **h** I've just been to the cinema.

2
- **a** I'm sitting down/working/studying/learning English.
- **b** I'm feeling tired/interested/bored/excited.
- **c** I wear a skirt and jumper/trousers and shirt/a dress.
- **d** I'm wearing ....
- **e** I come from ....
- **f** I'm a ...... (student/businessman/accountant/secretary).
- **g** I sit at a desk in my room.
- **h** How do you do?

3

Newspapers	Radio/TV
article	advert
advert	channel
crossword	interviewer
daily	live
editorial	local
evening	the news
front page	presenter
headline	soap opera
journalist	
local	
morning	
weekly	

4
adj - adjective   sing - singular
adv - adverb   v - verb
BA - Bachelor of Arts £ - pound
n - noun   1st - first
pl - plural   2nd - second

5 adverb
singular
adjective
tense
simple
pronoun
noun
article
plural
vocabulary

1 down - dictionary

Key

UNIT 3

Lesson 7

1. sang bought got was cost thought was went drank ate learnt made gave went took wrote

2.
   a The shop is closed.
   b The door is locked.
   c The film is finished.
   d English is spoken.

3. a checks b stripes c spots
   d diamonds e diagonals f circles
   g squares h curves i triangles
   j rectangles

4.
   a Tights are worn on the legs.
   b Gloves are worn on the hands.
   c T-shirts are not coats.
   d Jerseys have no trousers.
   e Hats are not long and thin.

5.
   a bites - tights
   b blouse - allows
   c clothes - chose, goes
   d coat - wrote
   e scarf - cough, laugh
   f rocks - box, logs
   g scissors - trousers
   h hot - what
   i these - peas, sees
   j why - lie

Lesson 8

1.
   a an unusual octagonal plate
   b a modern Japanese vase
   c a silver Bedouin bracelet
   d a small wooden antelope
   e a 22 carat gold ring
   f a cheap Japanese television
   g a white Swedish table
   h some round straw huts
   i a black leather suitcase
   j a cheap red book

2.
   a The village was flooded.
   b The rocks were moved.
   c The straw huts were damaged.
   d The treasure was washed away.
   e The skeleton coast was altered.
   f The Silver Pool was emptied.

3. alarm clock, clothes hanger, ironing board, shower curtain, tin opener, bottle opener, hair dryer, kitchen sink, table lamp, vacuum cleaner.

4. lakes pool mountains forests rivers deserts sea coast

5. Welcome start brought world first brought unusual open £20 advance

6. 'Treasure?' the old man asked in surprise. 'Yes,' I replied. 'I've got a map showing where it is.'
'Where is it? Where is it?' the old man asked.
'I'm not telling you,' I answered. 'I'm going to keep all the treasure for myself.'
'Really?' exclaimed the old man, 'then you don't know what the eighth clue is.'
'No I don't.' I said quickly. The old man smiled back. 'The eighth clue is that you'll never find the treasure alone.'

Lesson 9

1.
   a order   f order
   b request/order   g polite request
   c polite request   h order
   d polite request   i polite request
   e order   j order

2. will go, will give, will ask, will give, will return

3. a i   b iii or i   c ii   d i or ii

4.
   a A baker sells bread.
   b A photographer takes photographs.
   c An estate agent sells houses.
   d A greengrocer sells vegetables.
   e A mechanic mends cars.
   f A porter carries suitcases.
   g A secretary types letters.
   h A vet looks after sick animals.

5.
   1 The man in the picture is wearing glasses.
   2 The jumper is plain.
   3 There are no trousers on the chair.
   4 The desk only has two drawers.
   5 There are four books on the table.
   6 There is one bird outside the window.
   7 There is a pair of boots by the bed.
   8 There is nothing under the desk.
   9 There is nothing on the floor.
   10 His jacket has no pocket.

Key

UNIT 4

Lesson 10

1.
   - a the
   - b –
   - c a
   - d –
   - e –
   - f the
   - g –
   - h a
   - i the
   - j the
   - k a
   - l –
   - m the
   - n the
   - o a
   - p a

2. is called   means   can find   could want   offers   will miss

3.
   - a sauna
   - b rapids
   - c bowls
   - d snooker
   - e Solarium

4.
   - a Balcony
   - b Foyer
   - c Bar
   - d Stalls
   - e Stage
   - f Box Office

5.
   - a dancing
   - b working
   - c queuing
   - d smoke
   - e feeling
   - f thrill
   - g swim
   - h training

6.
   - a patio
   - b popular
   - c waterchute
   - d villas
   - e dome
   - f antique
   - g leisurely
   - h televisions

   1 down - paradise

Lesson 11

1. Possible answers:
   At eleven o'clock I'm going to have a beauty treatment.
   At twelve-thirty I'm going to have lunch.
   At two o'clock I'm going to walk in the woods.
   At three o'clock I'm going to windsurf.
   At four o'clock I'm going to have a riding lesson.
   At five o'clock I'm going to have English tea.
   At six o'clock I'm going to swim.
   At seven o'clock I'm going to eat supper.

2.
   - a I really love swimming in the river.
   - b Jeff enjoyed wind-surfing.
   - c I could watch tennis all day long but I hate playing it.
   - d Who prefers canoeing to cycling?
   - e Would you mind looking after my clothes?

3.
   - a table tennis
   - b tennis
   - c wind-surfing
   - d golf
   - e riding
   - f volley-ball
   - g badminton
   - h sailing
   - i canoeing

4.
   - a What's a Sauna? It's a kind of small hot room from Finland.
   - b What's a pedaloe? It's a kind of cycle on water.
   - c What are aerobics? It's a kind of exercise with music.
   - d What's a workout? It's a kind of individual exercise.
   - e What's a Turkish bath? It's a kind of large hot room with steam.

5.
   - a on
   - b about
   - c to
   - d to
   - e on, to
   - f with
   - g up
   - h on
   - i out
   - j up

6. to   for   choose   of   people   highly   things   eighteen   useful   plenty

Key

Lesson 12

1 a What does chilli con carne contain?
   b How do you make pizza?
   c Who likes hamburgers?
   d When do you drink port?
   e Why do the English like warm beer?
   f Where is tea grown?
   g Why do some people call it Coke?
   h How do you make tea?
   i Who invented Crêpes Suzettes?
   j Where does sherry come from?

2 a Soup is never the last course of the meal in England.
   b Fish and chips are always served hot in England.
   c Soft drinks never contain alcohol.
   d Green tea is never drunk with milk.
   e Paella in Spain always contains chicken and shell-fish.
   f Cheese fondue in Switzerland is always made at the table.
   g Sweet and sour pork is always served with rice or noodles in Chinese restaurants.

3 a meat, onion
   b meat, tomato, onion
   c pastry, meat, potato, minced
   d curry, goulash
   e desserts

4 fresh - frozen
   hard - soft
   hot - cold
   spicy - mild
   strong - weak
   thick - thin
   wet - dry
   whole - sliced

5 a fried   f lunch
   b boiled   g grilled
   c sliced bread h roast
   d toaster   i dinner
   e sandwich   j breakfast

   1 down = restaurant

6 a steak   d port
   b lamb   e cheese
   c beer   f pie

UNIT 5

Lesson 13

1 a this, this
   b those, that
   c that, the, that's, that's

2 Possible answers:

   a I didn't use to do homework all day.
   b My father didn't use to smoke a pipe.
   c My mother didn't use to drive a car.
   d I used to eat hamburgers.
   e I used to eat eggs.

3 a iv   d ii
   b v   e iii
   c i

4 don't never on with of doesn't who's isn't that so

5 at with with on in on in With in on

Lesson 14

1 a didn't she   e wasn't he
   b isn't he   f wouldn't you
   c aren't they   g doesn't it
   d wasn't it   h aren't they

2 a Does she like meeting and talking to people?
   b Is he happy at work?
   c Does she make people happy?
   d Did he use to be very rich?
   e Has she been on TV a lot?
   f Has he made a lot of films?
   g Does she help other people?
   h Was he born in March?
   i Do they both look happy?
   j Are you Scorpio?

3 bad-tempered - good-tempered, boring - interesting, careful - careless, friendly - unfriendly, honest - dishonest, kind - impatient, polite - rude, powerful - weak, thoughtful - thoughtless

4 a self-confident   d easy-going
   b bad-tempered   e good-tempered
   c open-minded

Key

5   a musical   f self-confident
     b childish   g sporty
     c romantic   h clever
     d cheerful   i angry
     e patient

1 down = character

Lesson 15

2   works, would like to visit, likes travelling, is studying, would like to meet, likes going, would like to, like swimming, would like to, would like to.

3   Eire - Ireland, Portugal - Portugal, España - Spain, France - France, Belgique - Belgium, Deutschland - Germany, Österreich - Austria, Nederland - Netherlands, Suisse - Switzerland, Danmark - Denmark, Norge - Norway, Sverige - Sweden, Suomi - Finland, Italia - Italy, Ellas - Greece.

4

```
T R A V E L L I N G
X E L P C I N E M A
P A P O E T R Y U F
O D B P C E B T S U
L I I E M R P D I R
I N S H I A R C O
T G F O O T B A L L
I P V W M U A M E Z
C S U K G R D A M P
S P O R T E F H K O
```

5

> Bell College
> Saffron Walden
> Essex CB11 3DP
>
> 5 October
>
> Dear Maria,
>
> I have just arrived at the college after a long journey. Everyone is so friendly and helpful that I feel at home already. Our classes today were great and I'm going to the disco tonight.
>
> Best wishes,
>
> Stefan

UNIT 6

Lesson 16

1   a The rice is washed with lots of water.
     b Then the rice is added to a saucepan of boiling water.
     c Next the saucepan is covered.
     d Then the rice is cooked for 8-11 minutes.
     e When there is no water left the rice is taken off the heat.
     f The rice is served immediately.

2   a thin nose   f short nose
     b round eyes   g square eyes
     c big eyes   h fat nose
     d long nose   i sad mouth
     e small eyes

3   a ear   f thumb
     b forehead   g forefinger
     c cheek   h nail
     d eyebrows   i palm
     e chin   j knuckle

4   out in in on in

5   a ii   d iii
     b iv   e i
     c v

Lesson 17

1   was had just taken went looked saw went told had seen went looked had seen

2   a walk under ladders
     b afraid of black cats
     c saw a UFO
     d what did it look like
     e always reading

3   a i tail ii whiskers iii head iv paws v claws
     b i horns ii hooves iii head iv tail
     c i gills ii tail iii head iv fins

4   a terrified   d enormous
     b bored   e tiny
     c large

Key

5 on in from off for on

6
- **a** gh - flight
- **b** h - heel
- **c** gh - thought
- **d** h - risk
- **e** gh - lighten
- **f** k - wife
- **g** gh - threw
- **h** gh - fly
- **i** b - jam

Lesson 18

1
- **a** 3
- **b** 6
- **c** 8
- **d** 4
- **e** 1
- **f** 7
- **g** 2
- **h** 5

2 cooked - tossed, mixed, dropped, locked, looked, worked
added - decided, haunted, interested
stirred - appeared, bored, closed, covered, disappeared

3
- **a** Beef comes from cows.
- **b** Butter is made from milk.
- **c** Eggs come from chickens.
- **d** Flour is made from wheat.
- **e** Lamb comes from sheep.
- **f** Oil is made from vegetables.
- **g** Pepper is hot.
- **h** Sugar is sweet.
- **i** Veal comes from calves.
- **j** Vinegar is sharp.

4
- **a** scales
- **b** rolling pin
- **c** knife
- **d** mixer
- **e** chopping board
- **f** toaster
- **g** spoon
- **h** sieve
- **i** tin opener
- **j** saucepan

5
cook   salt
bowl   recipe
whisk   pan
mixture   hole
oven   heat

6 eggs, butter, sugar
lemon,
year,
cheese, meat,

UNIT 7

Lesson 19

1
- **a** How often do you eat?
- **b** How many times do you eat fish?
- **c** What did you eat yesterday?
- **d** How healthy is your diet?
- **e** How often do you eat chocolate?
- **f** What were you like four years ago?
- **g** What kind of food do you like?
- **h** What did you like to eat?

2
- **a** smokes, eats
- **b** feels
- **c** had
- **d** cause
- **e** had
- **f** ate
- **g** get
- **h** was
- **i** feel
- **j** ate

3
- **a** onion
- **b** cucumber
- **c** tomato
- **d** peas
- **e** apple
- **f** banana
- **g** carrots
- **h** cabbage
- **i** grapes
- **j** oranges

4
- **a** v
- **b** iv
- **c** viii
- **d** iii
- **e** i
- **f** ii
- **g** vi
- **h** vii

5
- **a** bananas
- **b** chips
- **c** pasta
- **d** egg
- **e** ham
- **f** cake
- **g** tea
- **h** toast
- **i** rice
- 1 down = spaghetti

Key

Lesson 20

1.
   a was still smiling
   b ran/were running
   c only did
   d was doing
   e was thumbing
   f was playing
   g finished

2.
   a have never run
   b entered
   c started, have finished
   d has won
   e finished

3.
   a run
   b jog
   c walk
   d jump
   e sprint

4. mother - mum/mummy/ma
   father - papa/dad
   grandmother - nan/gran
   grandfather - granpa

5.
   a raked in
   b called off
   c go out
   d broke down
   e egged me on
   f cut down on
   g went off
   h dropped out
   i broke down
   j carried on

Lesson 21

1.
   a You must not drive faster than eighty kilometres an hour.
   b You must not turn left.
   c You must not overtake.
   d You must give way.
   e You must not turn right.
   f You must not enter.
   g You must not cycle.
   h You must not park.

2.
   a Find the picture described on page 75.
   b Use the interview with Mike Johnson printed on page 41.
   c Use the pancake recipe read in Lesson 18.
   d Look at the definitions included in Lesson 20.
   e Check the results of the survey done in Lesson 19.

3.
   a wood
   b mood
   c bone
   d foot
   e poured

4.
   a The Week
   b School Report
   c Mindbender
   d We're Fat And Lazy
   e Terrified At Midnight
   f Rock Me Now
   g My Kind Of Life
   h Hot And Tasty

5.
   ! exclamation mark
   " inverted commas
   - hyphen
   ' apostrophe
   ( ) brackets
   ; semi colon
   , comma
   . full stop
   ? question mark
   : colon

Key

UNIT 8

Lesson 22

1.
   a smallest
   b most beautiful
   c oldest
   d best
   e most exciting

2.
   a to take
   b to pack
   c swimming
   d getting
   e to take

3.
   a walking
   b windsurfing
   c beach
   d canoeing
   e climbing
   f birdwatching
   g miniature

4.
   a a sweet-smelling rose
   b a German-sounding name
   c an important-looking woman
   d a fast-moving game
   e a strong-tasting curry

5.
   a F
   b F
   c T
   d F
   e T
   f F

Lesson 23

1. had/took told went said thought took saw got

2.
   a Good boots are highly recommended.
   b The Portmeirion hotel is highly recommended.
   c Taking plenty of warm clothing is definitely advised.
   d Wearing jeans is not advised.
   e Camping is not permitted.

3.
   a bandage
   b aspirin
   c thermometer
   d plaster
   e scissors

4. special really always great absolutely expensive famous definitely

5.
   a whistle
   b hat
   c torch
   d spare food
   e hot drink
   f compass
   g sweaters
   h boots
   i gloves
   j first aid kit
   k sandwiches

   1 down = waterproofs.

Lesson 24

1.
   a York, with its marvellous shopping and excellent restaurants, is nearly two thousand years old and has something for everyone.
   b Saffron Walden, with a long history, is an attractive town near Cambridge.
   c Rio with over 4 million inhabitants is one of the largest cities in South America, covering an area of 60 square miles.
   d Stockholm, the capital of the old kingdom of Sweden, is built on 14 islands on the Baltic sea coast.
   e Basel, beautifully situated on the Rhine, is the second largest city with a population of 223,000.

2.
   a The poster should give general information.
   b Your group should contain no more than 4 people.
   c The poster should make our town look interesting.
   d The winning poster should attract tourists.
   e You should decide which tourist attractions to use.

3.
   a botanical gardens
   b Pubs
   c youth hostel
   d park
   e museum
   f art galleries
   g market

70

Key

4
- a fifteenth
- b twenty-first
- c eleventh
- d twentieth
- e nineteenth

5 for in over on by with in in of to

UNIT 9

Lesson 25

1
- a How long does it take to make an actor into a monster for 'Hellraiser II'?
- b Who chooses this week's 'Desert Island Discs'?
- c What's the morning story called?
- d What is 'My Country Right or Wrong' about?
- e When does 'You and Yours' finish?
- f What is on four times?
- g What is 'The Food Programme' about?

2
- a is 'The Morning Story' on?
- b is it called?
- c is 'Breakaway' about?
- d is 'Science Now' on?
- e is 'Out of Order' about?
- f is 'Music for Guitar' on?

3
- a mine
- b hers
- c theirs
- d ours
- e his

4
- a quizzes
- b the weather forecast
- c stories
- d comedy
- e pop music

5

10	ten	x	tenth
2	two	ii	second
4	four	iv	fourth
7	seven	vii	seventh
9	nine	ix	ninth
3	three	iii	third
5	five	v	fifth
8	eight	viii	eighth

6
- a 6.00, 9.00
- b 8.30
- c 6.00, 9.00, 12.10
- d 10.20
- e 10.50

Lesson 26

1
- a did you go
- b did you hide
- c did you begin

71

       d did you do
       e were you going to

2   **a** was told in the departure lounge.
       b was cut from its case.
       c was interviewed on his return to Earth.
       d was interviewed by satellite radio on Radio Earth.
       e was given a special job to do.

3   **a** stars   **d** satellite
       b rocket   **e** space shuttle
       c moon

4   **a** Detective Inspector Rawlings is about 1.8 metres tall.
       b Mount Everest is about 8708 metres high.
       c The speed limit is 48 kms an hour.
       d The distance is 90 metres.
       e The book is 7.5 cm thick.

5   at in of for in for by from for since

Lesson 27

1   **a** Have you heard the news?
       b Have you seen the producer?
       c Have you decided on the announcer?
       d Have you prepared your news items?
       e Have you recorded your programme?

2   has announced has been have closed have beaten has been said closed fell said beat

3   **a** editor
       b headmaster/mistress
       c Prime Minister
       d manager
       e captain
       f chef
       g manager/captain
       h manager

4   **a** tell   **f** say
       b tell   **g** told
       c say   **h** tell
       d told   **i** say
       e said   **j** telling

5   1 -a, 2 - f, 3 - d, 4 - c, 5 - g, 6 - b, 7 - e

UNIT 10

Lesson 28

1   **a** Madeleine asked Paul to visit her flat.
       b Madeleine asked Paul why he was seeing Sylvie.
       c Mary said something was wrong.
       d Frederick asked why Max was so afraid.
       e Clara said she hated Henry Blake.
       f Kay said drugs kill thousands of people every year.
       g Tony said the record company want us to make our first record.
       h Sam said she didn't want to go to the Opera Festival in Salzburg.
       i Sam said she wants to travel on her own.

2   **a** Clara thought that everything was going to be wonderful.
       b Madeleine thought that they were going to get married.
       c Beatriz said that they would try and help Max.
       d Kay said that she was going to expose the world of drugs.
       e Tony told the band that they were going to make a record.
       f Sam told her parents that she was going to spend the summer in Sardinia.

3   **a** calf
       b foal
       c kitten
       d lamb
       e puppy

4   audience - people
     bunch - keys
     flock - sheep
     herd - cows
     pack - cards

5   **a** thriller
       b horror
       c family
       d real life
       e animal
       f comedy
       g detective

Key

Lesson 29

1
- a The goose was also found by Peterson.
- b The tall man was attacked by a group of rough young men.
- c The shop window was broken by a stick.
- d A label was tied to the goose's leg.
- e The jewel was found inside the goose.
- f The Blue Carbuncle was stolen from the Hotel Cosmopolitan.
- g The robbery was discovered by James Ryder the assistant manager.
- h The jewel was kept in a desk in the bedroom.

2 The the The a a - a a an The

3 Christmas dinner, dining-room, hotel bedroom, language laboratory, language school, market place, newspaper cutting, newspaper story, sitting-room, under-manager

4
- a sneezing
- b coughed
- c crash
- d bang
- e screams
- f snore

5
- a away
- b back
- c after
- d round
- e out

6
- a One Pair of Eyes
- b Murder at Mortlock Hall
- c Rich Man, Poor Man
- d Dear Jan Love Ruth
- e Star for a Day
- f Frankenstein
- g The Boy Who Was Afraid

Lesson 30

1
- a Where is Frederick studying?
- b What kind of school is it?
- c Who is Beatriz?
- d What's the book called?
- e Where's Max from?
- f Why is he in England?
- g What did he do when he arrived?

2 d - 1, g - 2, k - 3, b - 4, i - 5, c - 6, f - 7, j - 8, e - 9, h - 10, a - 11

- a was, had died
- b saw
- c got, spoke
- d is, happened
- e looked, said
- f returned
- g had taken off, went
- h recognised
- i ran
- j approached, appeared
- k opened, had

3
- a do
- b make
- c do
- d make
- e doing
- f did
- g made
- h make
- i did, made
- j made

4
- a headmaster
- b students
- c computers
- d secondary
- e primary
- f laboratory
- g examinations
- h recording
- i university

1 down = education

5

language	which
baggage	approach
college	fetch
cottage	reach
edge	teach
judge	which